Weapons of Peace

Another Book by Mary Trask

The 12 Gemstones of Revelation

Availabe from Destiny Image Publishers

WEAPONS OF PEACE

God's Tools for Peace in a Chaotic World

MARY TRASK

 Please note that Destiny Image's publishing style capitalizes certain pronouns in Scripture that refer to the Father, Son, and Holy Spirit, and may differ from some publishers' styles. Take note that the name satan and related names are not capitalized. We choose not to acknowledge him, even to the point of violating grammatical rules.

Disclaimer: All emphasis within Scripture quotations is the author's own.

DESTINY IMAGE® PUBLISHERS, INC.
P.O. Box 310, Shippensburg, PA 17257-0310

"Speaking to the Purposes of God for This Generation and for the Generations to Come."

This book and all other Destiny Image, Revival Press, MercyPlace, Fresh Bread, Destiny Image Fiction, and Treasure House books are available at Christian bookstores and distributors worldwide.

For a U.S. bookstore nearest you, call 1-800-722-6774.
For more information on foreign distributors, call 717-532-3040.
Reach us on the Internet: www.destinyimage.com.

ISBN 13 Trade Paper: 978-0-7684-3668-6
ISBN 13 Hardcover: 978-0-7684-3669-3
ISBN 13 Large Print: 978-0-7684-3670-9
ISBN 13 Ebook: 978-0-7684-9031-2

For Worldwide Distribution, Printed in the U.S.A.
1 2 3 4 5 6 7 8 9 10 11 /14 13 12 11

DEDICATION

This book is dedicated to all my wonderful children and their families: Josh, Jenny, Claire, Avery, Noelle, Jeremiah, Valerie, Jordan, Kristi, Gil, Isaac, and Natalie. I love you all!

ACKNOWLEDGMENTS

I would like to thank my husband, John, for all the time invested in reading through my manuscript and releasing me to spend hours on end in the writing of this book. John, you're the best! Also, I would like to thank my dear friend, Maria, for all the joy and encouragement she has lavished upon me ever since we met. I am also very thankful to Ronda at Destiny Image for all the quick email responses and encouragement over this last year. You are a blessing!

ENDORSEMENTS

Mary Trask's book *Weapons of Peace* is much more than a treatise on the subject of peace. Mary combines her excellent gift of teaching God's Word with many personal testimonies and stories about the supernatural and miracles, as she pursued and possessed God's peace. From these experiences she demonstrates how the atmosphere, provision, and power of Heaven is released from a lifestyle of peace and rest. Thoroughly covering the subject of God's peace from many angles, Mary leads the reader through personalized summaries and prayer after each chapter to activate what has been taught. She provides tools to help renew the mind, align the heart and spirit with the truth of Scripture, attain personal victory over strongholds, and advance the Kingdom of Heaven through the increasing experience of God's peace daily. I highly recommend *Weapons of Peace!*

Michael Proctor
Senior Leader of Elisha's Request Ministries
Port Orchard, WA

God has given us a wonderful, powerful, and practical gift—a gift that often escapes notice among the many other aspects of our spiritual inheritance. Through winsome personal story telling and thoughtful Biblical exegesis, Mary Trask takes us on a journey of discovery and invites us to enroll in the Holy Spirit's school of peace. I encourage you to accept the invitation!

Gordon Anderson
Destiny City Church, Elder
Tacoma, WA

Weapons of Peace is a key for this generation. In the midst of so many things diverting our attention and causing anxiety, Mary brings us back to a foundational element that is essential in every believer's life. Mary has clearly and concisely identified the very thing that makes all of us thrive: living in the peace that was promised to us by Jesus through the Holy Spirit. *Weapons of Peace* is a must-read; it will equip you with keys to not only walk in peace, but also to impart and release it wherever you go.

Melissa Howe
Worship Leader, Bethel Church
Redding, CA

Mary Trask has written a must-read book for people desiring to apprehend and live in greater levels of God's peace. With real-life stories, *Weapons of Peace* clearly demonstrates, explains how to, and then practically leads readers to enjoy Heaven's peace here on earth, as well as how to generously release God's peace to everyone they encounter. This is one of those books I want to live!

Jerry Myhr
Pastor, Port Orchard Nazarene Church

True inner peace seems to be one of the rarest of human experiences. Although many may seek peace in a variance of outward circumstances, in Christ it is readily available. In her book, *Weapons of Peace,* Mary Trask has given us a clear and colorful picture of the power and peace we have in Peace, Himself. Many seek weapons of warfare that are carnal, yet Mary directs us to weapons of peace that already reside within us. There is a depth of tranquility and serenity that usurps all external influences when we recognize the weapons of peace the Lord has provided us. May you find a renewed revelation of the power that works within you as you read through the pages of this well-crafted book. Mary beautifully reminds us that Christ is able to do exceedingly and abundantly above what we can imagine or believe. As I read through *Weapons of Peace,* I was reminded of the abounding grace of the Lord to live restored, renewed, and daily revived. I was reminded that regardless of the world of challenges and uncertainties that may be around us, we have a peace the world cannot give, a peace that dwells, rules, umpires, and directs our lives. This truly is one of our greatest weapons.

Doug Stringer
Founder/President
Somebody Cares America/International
Turning Point Ministries International

We live in interesting times; in fact, more is written in the Word about the endtimes than any other time. How will believers function in such a turmoil-filled world? With all the pressures of a world falling apart, how will believers accomplish and even thrive in fulfilling the Father's will, bringing in the greatest harvest the world has ever known? Mary Trask gives one tremendous clue in *Weapons of Peace.* Christians the world over will have to understand the magnitude this promised peace is to play in order for them to not be overtaken in the tumultuous times that are heading our way.

Kurt Snyder
Senior Pastor, Destiny City Church
Tacoma, WA
www.destinycitychurch.org

CONTENTS

FOREWORD

Do you struggle sometimes with anxiety, fear, or stress? Are there times in your life when you "lose it" under pressure and wonder afterward what exactly happened to produce such an intense reaction? Have you ever suffered from migraines, high blood pressure, muscle tension, digestive disorders, depression, and other health conditions? You are not alone. We live in a world full of intense schedules, deadlines, conflicts, and crises. We live in a world full of elements that challenge our peace.

Weapons of Peace is a timely message. Jesus wants you to live in His glorious peace in the midst of storms, crises, and pressures. When everything around you is being shaken, there is a place for you to stand, a place for you to rest, a place of perfect peace!

I remember a time years ago when my world was being rocked. Pressures surrounded me, and I carried so much stress over it. One day while weeping before the Lord in a place of prayer, I heard Him speak these profound words: "There is nothing in this life worth being anxious about." It felt like a shaft of light entered my heart when I heard these life-changing words. The reality of this truth filled me, and I began to think things like, "Well of course! Worrying isn't going to change anything! I am in the trial of my life right now, but being anxious is not going to fix it! Jesus is greater than anything I am facing!" Suddenly the tangible presence of peace filled my entire being. I was introduced that day to the peace of God.

Following this moment of deliverance, I randomly opened my Bible to find somewhere to read and it opened to Philippians 4:6-8 NASB:

> *Be anxious for nothing, but in everything by prayer and supplication with thanksgiving let your requests be made known to God.*
>
> *And the peace of God, which surpasses all comprehension, will guard your hearts and your minds in Christ Jesus.*
>
> *Finally, brethren, whatever is true, whatever is honorable, whatever is right, whatever is pure, whatever is lovely, whatever is of good repute, if there is any excellence and if anything worthy of praise, dwell on these things.*

God had not only visited me with His peace, but He gave me instruction on how to live in it.

I then got up to do some chores. While I was driving downtown, I turned on the tape player (yes, we actually used tapes back then), and immediately heard the following words being sung, "If He carries the weight of the world on His shoulder, My sister, He is able to carry you through." Another wave of that blessed peace filled me. I was so amazed at the faithfulness of God. Oh, how good He is!

I got through that time in my life and many more times of crisis and pressure since that day by acknowledging and receiving the peace of God. Jesus is the Prince of Peace, and He is so committed to stilling the storms for us and granting us a place in His presence where all is at rest.

You will glean insights from *Weapons of Peace* that will help you through life. It is a book that you can use in your devotion times or put in strategic places for others to read. These will give you encouragement and keys to abiding in His peace.

In John 20:19 and 21, Jesus said to His disciples, *"Peace be with you."* Right now, two thousand years later, Jesus lovingly says to you too, *"Peace be with you."*

Receive His peace. He came that you would encounter it.

Patricia King
Founder of XP Media
and host of *Extreme Prophetic Television*

INTRODUCTION

The sun shone brightly that day as three young women engaged in small talk, each in her perfectly tailored ensemble with matching clutch held tightly under her arm. The friends laughed as their thin high heels clicked in an irregular pattern on the pavement. Their work day had finally ended, and they only had a short bus ride to the "women only" apartments where they resided.

Suddenly, a group of naval officers turned the corner heading directly toward the giddy group. Of the three handsome young men, one red-headed officer stood out in Betty's mind as she flashed a smile in his direction. Instead of continuing his march with the other sharply dressed officers, Charlie made an about turn and approached her. He was definitely interested in the auburn-haired beauty.

Charlie and Betty were eventually married in 1952.

The following year, their firstborn son made his entrance into the world, followed by a daughter several years later. This, however, was not the end for this growing family. Eventually eight more children joined the family, five boys and five girls altogether. One would think that with a family that size, they all would be vivacious and outgoing. However, that was not the case with one daughter in particular…me!

As the second oldest in the family and the oldest girl, many responsibilities fell into my lap. My sister Teri and I were often given the baby to change or feed, depending on his or her needs at the moment, while my mother scurried around caring for the growing number of children within our household. Dad, who worked many long hours at the office, came home to a house full of bikes, books, and basketballs. His neat and tidy world suddenly became chaotic and overwhelming at times. His response was to bring order as best he could.

In our younger years, before Dad arrived home, the household clutter had to be picked up, the table set, the food ready, and each of us prepared to sit in our assigned seats for dinner. After prayers for the meal were offered up, we each were given five minutes to describe the highlights of our day. As we grew older and he grew mellower, the stiffness lifted and we found ourselves chattering happily with each other about the day's activities around the dinner table.

My mother, gifted in hospitality, often found herself faced with the feat of trying to feed an army! She not only had our regular 12, but often had friends, visitors, and even exchange students who joined us at our growing table. Consequently, she became very skilled at cooking in bulk and then praying that God would multiply what she prepared to fill the stomachs of all present. I never remember going hungry as God always provided for us in a multitude of ways.

This was my world.

At home surrounded by my siblings, I felt confident and quite capable. I knew what to expect. My world felt safe and secure. However, outside the confines of our house and backyard, fear took hold of me, causing me to withdraw in reservation. As I had plenty of playmates within the home, neighborhood friends were optional. Only if my younger sister went out first to establish contact would I consider joining her on the next visit.

My mother stated that even as an infant, if I heard an unfamiliar voice on the radio, I would begin crying. As a toddler, any time a stranger came to the front door, I immediately took cover under her skirt and had to be coaxed out. As my father's job required our family to move a number of times throughout California, I was forced to start a new school and try to establish friends again in a new location.

Every time I started my school day, the same fears were always there to greet me. In the early years, I tried to be as "invisible" as possible in order to avoid as much interaction as possible. One elementary teacher even reported that I appeared to be a rather melancholy child who seldom smiled in the classroom.

Fear had me in lockdown.

Later, much of my significance came in performing well academically and in athletic endeavors; however, my real joy came when I discovered my creative flair for writing. In writing, I could express myself freely and without inhibitions. Fantasy and daydreaming became forms of escape as well. In both middle school and high school, I discovered drama, where I could temporarily step out of my prison of fear and be "transformed" into someone else.

It was only after I had a dramatic encounter with Jesus Christ at age 15 that my confidence in His power and authority began to break off the chains of fear holding me back in so many areas. Though the initial fears diminished, I still had many internal battles that robbed me of much joy throughout my early years as a Christian.

Fear kept me thinking as an unbeliever at times. Fear tried convincing me that it was all right to worry and fret. Fear often wanted me to hide and cover up so I could maintain a good image rather than exposing my true self and allowing the Truth to heal me from the inside out. Fear of rejection pushed me into developing a judgmental spirit rather than one of love and acceptance. By criticizing others, I found I felt a little bit better about myself.

"At least I'm not as bad as so-and-so," I used to think to myself.

Such a lie!

Today as I look at the world around me, I have come to understand that many others are also struggling with the same type of imbedded fears as I had. The Bible indicates that in the endtimes people's hearts will fail them *"from fear and the expectation of those things which are coming on the earth, for the powers of the heavens will be shaken"* (Luke 21:26). The American Heart Association, in their 2009 updated report, states that of the American population, 36.3 percent in the year 2006 experienced some kind of coronary heart disease.[1] These statistics tell us that nearly one out of every three people living in the United States has experienced some type of heart disease or stroke! Not all heart disease is a result of fear; however, the stresses faced by the upcoming generation differ in many ways from those of their predecessors and fears regarding provision seem to be high on the list. Stress-related anxieties plague so many around us that it seems almost commonplace for many people to be on some kind of anti-depressant.

Some are able to temporarily "overpower" their fears by relying on alcohol consumption to help them relax and numb the pain of life. Others find that drugs, both legal and illegal, are able to alleviate a portion of their fears and worries for a time until, in a sober moment, they find the reality of their broken world crashing in around them. Still others have found the adrenaline rush of sports, entertainment, and other distractions as their preferred method for avoiding the fears that are constantly simmering in the backs of their minds.

Performance-driven lists of "must-do" activities in hopes of achieving "the best" in child-rearing and education drive both parents and children to a busy, high-paced lifestyle that leaves little time for establishing dwelling places filled with the peace of God. Everyone is on the run in different directions to some commitment or another. Our full schedules cause us to only add to the increasing amounts of pressure and fear found in today's society.

Chronic sleeplessness is another indicator that worries or fears have taken hold in our lives. Psalm 127:1-2 says:

> *Unless the Lord builds the house, they labor in vain who build it; unless the Lord guards the city, the watchman stays awake in vain. It is vain for you to rise up early, to sit up late, to eat the bread of sorrows; for so He gives His beloved sleep.*

These verses indicate that unless the Lord builds or sets up our homes, all that we do is in vain, no matter how hard we try by staying up late or getting up early! Peaceful sleep, we're told, is promised to those fully trusting or resting in the Lord. In my own life, I have found sleeplessness is a good indicator that fear or worry has crept back in!

The shaking "sands" of this world's economy is not something that should totally surprise us as we are told in Hebrews 12:27 that the Lord Himself is shaking everything that can be shaken in order to remove or topple those things not solidly established upon the rock. It is His desire to allow the world to clearly recognize those things that remain solid and eternally enduring, namely, our faith in Jesus and the promises given to us, His people.

This is why we must cultivate peace in our lives in order to endure the increased shakings in the days ahead!

As a Christian, I slowly began to understand that somehow I should not give in to fear, but instead I was exhorted to walk in peace. However, though I could see what I needed to do, actually being able to walk in peace was a task I found next to impossible. Fear regularly managed to rob me of my joy, pulling me back in its clutches.

How many times have we as Christians declared we believe the promises of God and yet with our own lips confessed fear or worry over our loved ones? As they go out the door, we say "Be careful!" or "Take care!" In saying that, it seems we are declaring that they should be filled with care or worries throughout the day. Philippians 4:6 in the King James Version says *"Be careful for nothing"* and yet I still catch myself continuing to say "be careful" more times than I like to admit.

Though I may have tried to avoid it, some of my actions and words fed fear into the lives of my children at times, especially our youngest. They saw me worry about them and their activities. Sometimes I allowed my own fearful imaginations to take hold of me, and I responded in panic. My times of fear influenced my husband and hindered his ability to make wise decisions for our family.

†

Only the supernatural peace of God can hold us steady in shaky times.

I desperately needed the peace of God—not just a temporary peace, but one that would endure and persist even through the most challenging of times. It's only been in the last several years during an in-depth study of peace in the Bible that I finally grasped both the power and the importance of this amazing gift given to us by Jesus, as indicated in John 14:27.

> *Peace I leave with you, my peace I give to you; not as the world gives do I give to you. Let not your heart be troubled, neither let it be afraid.*

As I pondered this verse, I realized three important truths were described here.

1. Jesus gave us each the gift of His peace for a reason.

2. The peace of God is completely different from the world's version of "peace."

3. We were instructed not to allow our hearts to be troubled or afraid.

Naturally, more questions arose in my mind.

What was the purpose of this peace? How are we to use this gift? What is the difference between the peace of God and the world's peace? Why are we told not to allow fear or worry in our lives? How do we do this? What role does peace play in the Kingdom of God? Also, how important is this gift of peace in the chaotic and peace-starved world we live in today?

As I began my search, I was excited by what I found. With my own personal struggles with fear still fresh in my mind, I began to understand this gift as a key weapon given to us by Jesus for "shaky" times such as these. Without His peace, we would have little hope of effectively walking as mature believers in the Kingdom of God.

In order to explore the types and purposes of peace found in the Bible, we first need to understand how peace is an integral part of the Kingdom of God and an important portion of the very essence of our God: Father, Son, and Holy Spirit. Once we understand how peace functions in the Godhead, we then can follow the steps laid out for us in Scripture so we can access God's peace, allowing us to remain in perfect harmony with Heaven even while living on this chaotic globe.

Chapter 1

THE KINGDOM OF PEACE WITHIN US

The meeting had ended. People stood up from their tables and began helping with the cleanup process. Small groups of believers visited briefly together in between the hustle and bustle of folding tables and chairs being returned to their places of storage. In the middle of this busyness, a young mother tried to convince my friend and me that she was "fine" even while tears welled up in her eyes.

We both knew things were not "fine" and she needed some time to be covered in prayer. Pulling her into a quieter room, we sat down and began asking questions.

Fear and prayerlessness were the culprits.

Diagnostic questions helped us in discerning the exact source of the lies she had entertained. Fear of abandonment, anxiety, and worry all played their roles in robbing her of any type of peace. She felt herself on the edge of "losing it."

Once the lies perpetrated by fear were identified, we led her in a prayer to first confess her sin in believing the lies, and then we had her address the source of those lies and cast them out. After devising some plans to take positive steps in the opposite direction of these fears, we closed in prayer.

She felt much better and was at peace once again.

By the time we had finished, nearly everyone had already left the church. Only a few lights were left on so we exited through the back door. The other two ladies headed for their cars and then noticed that I was walking home in the dark. Though my house was only a hundred yards away, they both expressed concern for my safety and wanted to drive me to my front door. They had noticed a number of cars still parked in our lot from a nearby high school football game and a few "strangers" wandering toward their vehicles.

As sweet as their offer appeared to be, I had to laugh. After coming from a room filled with the presence of the Holy Spirit, I felt completely covered and safe in His glory. I knew the angels of the Lord were close by.

No. There was nothing to fear.

As I walked the short distance home, I realized that they probably had not fully experienced the confident assurance one feels when you are living in the peace of God. Isaiah 32:17-18 says:

> *The work of righteousness will be peace and the effect of righteousness, quietness and assurance forever. My people will dwell in a peaceful habitation, in secure dwellings and in quiet resting places.*

The very essence of the Godhead is one of peace; He is one who desires peace with all humankind. Jehovah Shalom (the Lord is Peace) is the name given by Gideon to the place where an altar was built to worship God (see Judg. 6:24). Jesus is referred to as the Prince of Peace in Isaiah 9:6, and the Holy Spirit is referred to as the Comforter in John 14:26. The word *comfort* is defined as "imploration, solace, comfort, consolation" and is further defined as "to call near, invite, invoke, to call for."[1]

It seems odd that even while the Creator of the universe has already declared the way of peace, the world seems determined to ignore this gift and instead tries to create its own version of "peace." Numerous "peace talks" around the world seem to only bring about a false or momentary sense of relief while all the time the eternal way of peace literally stares us in the face.

While traversing through passages of the Old Testament, we can find many references to this "shalom" peace[2] in connection with the Kingdom of God and with His people. Psalm 122:6 exhorts us to pray for the peace of Jerusalem, and later

Haggai 2:9 describes the glorious latter temple as a place where peace will be given by God.

(When we look at the pictorial language given to us in Revelation 21, we are reminded in verses 2, 9, and 10 that Jerusalem is not only a symbol of Israel, but also the glorious Bride of Christ. So in essence, when we pray for the peace of Jerusalem, we are praying for peace to come on the city and upon both Jews and Gentiles comprising the Bride of Christ!)

Other Old Testament promises describe ways of pleasantness and paths of peace offered to us by Wisdom, according to Proverbs 3:17. Perfect or complete peace is promised to those whose minds are stayed upon the Lord (see Isa. 26:3). Psalm 85:8 indicates that the Lord will speak peace to His people and His saints.

As we further examine this "peaceful habitation" for the people of God, spoken of in Isaiah 32:17, we are also reminded by the words of Jesus in Luke 17:21 that *"the kingdom of God is within"* us. By combining these two truths together, we can see that God's work of righteousness *within us* is what brings about quietness, assurance, secure dwellings, and quiet resting places. In other words, even if we lived in war-torn regions of the world, the promises of God are quite clear. He continues to offer us "green pastures" and "still waters" of refreshment while bathing our weary spirits with His peace. The comfort of the Holy Spirit is what gives us direction for our steps through any *"valley of the shadow of death"* (see Ps. 23:4).

Helen Keller, an American author, political activist, and lecturer, once spoke about this kind of peace. She said:

> I do not want the peace which passeth understanding, I want the understanding which bringeth peace.[3]

It is my belief that the Lord does want to bring us to a place of understanding as to how we can walk in His peace, though the gift of peace He offers us far surpasses all human understanding and logic at times (see Phil. 4:6-7). This peace cannot be explained in human terminology. It is a gift from the God of peace, if we are first willing to lay down all our "stuff" in order to receive it from Him.

I have experienced this peace, even while moving into a house located right on the border of two rival gangs. Though this house was not one we might have chosen had our circumstances been different, it was the only one available that fit within our limited, one-income household. A dear friend offered us the house, which included many mature fruit trees and a huge back lot where our children were able to play freely. It was only after we moved in that we came to fully understand the precarious location of this home! The bullet hole in the front window was a constant reminder that guns did go off at times in our neighborhood. We even joked about having "drive-by drills," in which the children would suddenly drop to the floor. In addition to all this, John, my husband, had to work the graveyard shift, leaving me and our four children at home in the evenings. This was the time when many gang conflicts would occur.

I had to make a choice. Either I would live in continual fear, causing our children to be crippled by my decisions, or I could demonstrate that I truly did believe the Lord was able to protect us.

†

Receiving God's gift of internal peace is a choice we each must make for ourselves.

The grace of God totally covered us in our decision to trust Him.

One morning while living in our own gang-filled corner of the world, I felt the need to go out in our front yard to sweep the scattering of dead leaves that covered our driveway. As I swept, I noticed a familiar face walking down the sidewalk in front of our house.

It was the neighborhood satanist, Jeff,[4] who lived only three doors down from us. It was rumored that he regularly held meetings that included animal sacrifices. His sister, belonging to one of the gangs, was often gone or busy. His 5-year-old nephew, Damian, came to our house daily, often knocking on our door as soon as the sun peeked in the horizon and spending the entire day with us rather than returning to their home where Jeff resided.

Jeff's unintelligible muttering stopped when he saw me standing on the driveway. Silently, he stared, causing me to return his looks of curiosity. Our eyes met.

"You're not scared of me, are you?" he asked.

"No," I responded. Prior to our meeting, I had just come out of several hours of prayer and fellowship with the King of kings. The peace of the Kingdom was all over me.

His silent gaze continued for a few more moments. Puzzled by my stance, he continued.

"I see that you know God."

"Yes, I do," I smiled. "I know Him very well."

Jeff's eyes seem to scan the atmosphere surrounding me.

"I see a light, an aura shining around you."

"That's the light of Jesus Christ," I explained.

With that statement, he had heard enough and continued muttering down the street just as he had before our conversation.

On another occasion, two of our sons were climbing the tree in our front yard when Jeff happened to pass by again while heading to the park just blocks from our house. He stopped, looked up in the tree, and called to our preteen boys.

"I am Jesus Christ! Worship me!"

The boys, unimpressed with his false claims, began to laugh spontaneously. They couldn't help themselves! They knew the truth and couldn't be shaken by someone attempting to tell them otherwise.

Realizing his words had no impact upon them, he continued down the sidewalk, apparently undeterred by their response. Several years later, after they had moved away (their house burned down!), we happened to run into Jeff at a local park. Our family and other friends held "church" in "Hobo Park" each Sunday by offering a warm meal, some basic supplies, and words of encouragement to those finding themselves in desperate living circumstances. Hundreds would show up unexpectedly as we ministered both in song and in the preaching of the Word. Though many homeless people had simply gathered for the free food we were offering, they were also given the opportunity to respond to the good news of Jesus.

When he spotted us, Jeff excitedly approached to inform us that his nephews were in the area and would want to see us again. Unfortunately that meeting never materialized; however, we still believe our example had an impact upon his life and those of his extended family. Someday, we may be pleasantly surprised to find that, in response to all our prayers, they have all come to know Jesus Christ as well!

The path I chose to walk during this particular season of our lives proved to be the right one. I did experience peace, though there were still many areas I had yet to conquer. The peace He gave me enabled me to sleep at night knowing that my Heavenly Father had set up His angels to stand guard over us each night for the year or so that we lived in that small two-bedroom house.

Yes, I could have stayed up all night trying to watch out the window for any signs of gang activity, but the lack of sleep and the stress from trying to carry that load would have made me sick! It was too much for me to bear so I gave all my cares and worries to the Lord.

Fretting Causes Harm

King David himself must have had some experience with worry as he tells us in Psalm 37:8, *"...do not fret—it only causes harm."* Later in his writings, he makes reference to the meek inheriting the earth and delighting themselves in the abundance of peace (see Ps. 37:9,11). Somehow I suspect he was all too familiar with the sickening churn of his stomach whenever panic or fear set in. Yet I believe David eventually learned the secret of casting his burdens upon the Lord as Psalm 37:11 speaks not simply of peace, but actually an *abundance* of peace! Imagine the depth of peace he had the opportunity to develop while spending years in the wilderness hiding from a spiritually tormented king who was continually trying to kill him!

So, how accurate is Psalm 37:8 when it indicates that stress and fear actually cause us harm? Pastor Henry W. Wright, a third-generation minister with a successful healing ministry, states in his book, *A More Excellent Way: Be in Health,* that he has been able to identify at least 43 different diseases and illnesses with their root causes stemming from the effects of fear and stress![5]

With statistics like that and the reported fears and stresses that so many Christians seem to encounter in today's modern society, one may begin to wonder if verses like Romans 14:17 could still be true. It says:

> *For the kingdom of God is not eating and drinking, but righteousness and peace and joy in the Holy Spirit.*

As contradictory as it may appear in lieu of our many life experiences, God's Word is infallible and therefore cannot be wrong. We must acknowledge, as the truthfulness of this verse indicates, that something in our own lives must be out of alignment with what God has intended for us. It is up to us to discover what hindrances to peace we have allowed in, remove them, and then learn how to release the abundance of peace promised to us in our everyday lives.

I believe a key to unlocking the source of our misunderstanding may be found in Hebrews chapters 3 and 4. In chapter 3, verse 11, the writer of Hebrews states that the Lord declares that a rebellious generation of Israel would not enter into His rest (see Heb. 3:7-11; Ps. 95:7-11). The Greek word used for this "rest" describes a "reposing down, abode, to settle down, colonize, to desist, and also refers to sabbatism or Sabbath."[6]

This struck me as curious when I realized the whole nation of Israel was faithfully observing their Sabbath day of rest as directed by Moses and the Ten Commandments. They had to follow this direction for Sabbath rest as their daily supply of manna would not even be available on the day of Sabbath. Obviously, these verses must have referred to a different type of rest that the children of Israel had never achieved!

As we read through both chapters 3 and 4 of Hebrews, we notice some pretty strong language encouraging us to take hold of this rest. The writer says in Hebrews 3:12-13:

> ***Beware*** *brethren, lest there be in any of you an evil heart of unbelief in departing from the living God; but* ***exhort*** *one another daily, while it is called "Today," lest any of you be hardened through the deceitfulness of sin.*

Then he says, *"...let us* ***fear*** *lest any of you seem to have come short of it"* (Heb. 4:1). And Hebrews 4:11 tells us that we must be *diligent* to enter that rest.

So why do you think this rest was considered so important?

To help unlock the significance behind this true Sabbath rest, we need to look at Hebrews 4:9-10. It says:

> *There remains therefore a rest for the people of God. For he who has entered His rest has himself also ceased from his works as God did from His.*

The previous verses mentioned in Hebrews spoke of the need for diligence to enter into the rest of God, and yet Hebrews 4:9-10 clearly says this true Sabbath rest requires a ceasing of all our own efforts. By putting these verses together, we can begin to see that the works and striving of our flesh must end so that we can learn how to rest in the Lord. When we stop all our efforts, the Holy Spirit is allowed to intervene, guiding and directing our every step.

This new form of Sabbath rest is not one that is limited to one day out of seven. It is a rest or state of peace that the Lord desires each of us to remain in constantly as His gift to us!

The Father's call for us to cease from our labors is for the purpose of initiating intimate fellowship with Him. Jesus came to demonstrate this way of peace while living on earth. The Holy Spirit was then released to help guide and direct us into these paths of peace.

So, as the writer of Hebrews indicates, it is time for us to diligently learn this way of true Sabbath rest. In learning the secrets of rest, we will also discover the weapons of peace left here on earth for our use. These weapons will not only release peace in our own lives, but will also establish peace in the hearts of others and release peace into our realms of influence.

◆ ◆ ◆

Paths of Peace

To begin our labors of truly entering into His peace, one must first start by asking for God's gift of peace. Though realizing we each need peace, we must also understand that there will be a season of training that must take place as we learn how to walk and remain upon these paths of peace mentioned throughout the Word of God.

Mastering the mental disciplines necessary to achieve and maintain God's peace in our lives is something I first noticed as gravely lacking in my own heart. However, once I understood what was needed to carefully guard my heart in this area, the peace I sought gradually became easier to achieve through the empowering of the Holy Spirit.

The principle of asking in prayer for whatever we lack must be utilized, and then as we ask, seek, and knock, we'll find the Holy Spirit more than willing to pour out in abundance to cover all our weakness (see Matt. 7:8).

Let's Pray

Lord Jesus, I come before You recognizing my own lack in the area of peace. I admit I don't fully understand what it means to work diligently to enter into Your rest, so I ask that You speak to my heart and teach me Your ways in this area. Open my mind and help me to really comprehend all You desire to teach me. Help me not to just understand these truths, but help me to actually apply and walk in these new paths of peace. I'm tired of living a life full of stress and worry. Forgive me for believing the lies of the enemy and allowing these things to rob me of my joy in You. Wash me in Your blood and grant me the grace to press forward in diligently learning all I need in this area.

Right now, I come against any hindering spirit that would try to distract or rob me of these truths! I bind you and command you to leave me now! I will receive the peace of God in my heart and mind. I will understand and practice the mental disciplines I need to overcome all fear and worry. I declare all this in the name of Jesus!

Holy Spirit, I invite You to flood me with more of Your grace and peace so I can press on to receive everything I need to conquer fear.

Thank you for hearing and answering my prayers! Amen.

Chapter 2

THE SWORD OF PEACE

There was a time when our family had the opportunity to live at a 600-acre ranch with a herd of 30 to 40 horses. The ranch had been donated to a Christian group that turned the entire place into a Christian family camp that integrated a riding and horsemanship program as a part of their outreach into surrounding communities.

While seeking employment, John ended up being hired as one of the maintenance people for the campgrounds. As one of the "perks," they offered us the opportunity to come and live on the ranch. Eager for the children to experience ranch life, we ended up driving our customized two-level motor home up to the camp and lived there for more than a year.

Our "customized" motor home resulted when John added a four-foot high room on top so he and I could have our own space. He did a very nice job in matching the siding to make it look nice inside and out, but we had many heads turning asking us what kind of motor home it was!

We made the move to Wolf Mountain and found great joy in exploring trails, swimming in their pool, riding bikes around the camp, collecting wildflowers, and enjoying the horses. For most of the time at camp, the children were able to play around the motor home, reveling in the outdoors, but when winter hit, I had to become extremely creative in finding ways to entertain our four very active children.

One of the great joys we had during the bustling summer months was the opportunity to minister to the many counselors hired for that season. Often we'd find our little motor home crowded with spiritually-hungry young adults who found their way to our door. I can still remember seeing every free spot taken in the front portion of our motor home with staff and counselors asking us about some deeper truths in the Kingdom of God. As our children slept in the back with the door shut, we prayed and ministered sometimes until well past midnight. What fun!

Often the older two boys, Jeremiah, age 8, and Joshua, age 9, were permitted to ride their bikes down the hill to our closest neighbor (about a mile away) where they could play with other children the same age as them. Unfortunately, the younger two children, Jordan, age 5, and Natalie, age 3, were forced to stay close to our motor home so I could watch them.

There was, however, one particular day when I felt as though the very core of my confidence in God was tested. The day had begun as normal. John had left for work on the grounds somewhere. The children had eaten, and the older ones were begging me to release them so they could head out on their bikes and visit their friends.

I agreed, reminding them to return before lunch. Happily, they sped away, leaving Jordan and Natalie for me to entertain. The younger children colored for a while and watched a short video before Jordan announced that he was bored and wanted to go for a walk. That morning I was in the middle of baking and couldn't leave. My free-spirited son, however, could not be persuaded to play a game or some other activity that would keep them close by.

Finally after much discussion, I decided that both Natalie and Jordan could be permitted to take a short walk across the meadow to the road directly down the hill from us, past the small grove of trees and then back up the gravel road leading to our motor home. The whole walk should have taken maybe five or ten minutes, depending on how many pebbles they stopped to pick up or the amount of wildflowers they felt inclined to collect.

After clearly going through all their instructions so they understood the plan, I released the children to take their short walk while I finished up in the motor home. Their course allowed me to see them nearly the entire time, until they disappeared behind the grove of trees, but I knew that I would soon see their little faces emerging on the other side.

I'm not sure exactly what had distracted me, but each time I looked up checking for the children, they were not where I expected them to be.

"Oh, they must have stopped to play with something behind the trees," I told myself as I quickly finished up my project.

Finally, after about 20 minutes, I decided I had better go and round up my little explorers. I wandered down the gravel road to meet up with them, but when I got to the grove of trees they were no where to be seen! My heart began to race a bit as I called out their names.

No answer.

Hurriedly, I rushed to several of the nearby trails and called out again.

Still no answer!

Without a lot of skill in maintaining my peace, all kinds of thoughts began flooding my mind. Had they fallen into the nearby well, which had been opened for repairs? Did they wander over to the open irrigation canal with its swift-flowing waters? There were so many places and directions they could have gone. I didn't know where to begin in my search!

As these days were prior to cell phones and we had no phone lines connected to the motor home, I was unable to call John or anyone else for help. I began to pray in desperation under my breath.

Just then, I saw our two older boys returning on their bikes, coming over the hill. Quickly, I explained to them the situation and sent each of them off in a different direction on their bikes, while I jumped on my own bike and started down a different trail in hopes of running into Jordan and Natalie.

As the minutes passed by, the more fearful and panicked I became. Tears ran down my cheeks as I quickly scanned the canal looking for any indication that our children had been on the trail.

I saw nothing until I came across a dead deer partially blocking the trail. Maneuvering my bicycle around the carcass, I continued my ride to the top of the ridge, now breathless and fear-bound.

Still no sign of the children!

I decided to head back down the hill toward our motor home to see if either of our two sons had been successful in their search. As I got closer to our spot, I suddenly noticed four young children, two of them with bikes, walking down the road toward home.

By the time I reached our children, I was nearly hysterical with joy and relief. I couldn't help but cry as I hugged our two little adventurers. Yes, I probably should have spanked our 5-year-old, as he had initiated the whole escapade, but I was so happy to see them all I could muster up was a strong verbal warning that he had better not do that ever again!

When the children started off, they had fully intended on following my directions for their little walk. But the day was so beautiful that Jordan was not ready to end their hike when they reached the end of the grove so he convinced Natalie that they should not return to the motor home so soon.

With Jordan in the lead, they simply continued walking on the road from behind the grove straight up the hill. (They must have made their escape in a moment when my attention was directed elsewhere!) When they arrived at the top of the hill, Jordan then decided to take the trail alongside the irrigation canal.

Our 3-year-old was a bit hesitant, but our fearless 5-year-old had confidence enough for them both! Without a moment of uncertainty, Jordan led Natalie down the familiar path our family had often taken for hikes. Things were going well until they came across the dead deer. The sight of the putrid-smelling carcass covered in flies sent Natalie into tears. She wanted to go home!

Unable to persuade her otherwise, the two turned around and began their trek back home. That was when their older brother, Josh, discovered the two wayward travelers and heroically led them back to safety.

Now you may be wondering how any of this has anything to do with the establishment of peace? Let me explain.

If we were to compare the safe trail I had laid out for our young children to walk upon to the paths of peace the Holy Spirit calls us to remain upon, we can begin to see a clear lesson in all this. The paths of peace were designed with our safety in mind. Peace was meant to help guard and protect our minds from the mental assaults of the enemy.

When we choose to listen to lies about God, ourselves, and others, we often find ourselves being led in the opposite direction from peace. The joy and grace lift as we wander farther and farther from what the Spirit of God intended. Often our breaking point comes when we run across evidence of death and decay in our lives as a result of our sin. (The dead deer!)

†

By mentally agreeing with lies, we can easily be led off the paths of peace.

Once we recognize sin and the impact it has on our lives, the goodness of God offers each of us a way of escape. We can choose to exercise the sweet gift of repentance by confessing our sins and failures, accepting God's gift of forgiveness, and rebuking any spirit behind those lies. Once the lie and the spirit behind that lie are removed, we can be led back to the paths of peace where we belong.

My simple scenario depicting the importance of remaining on the designated paths of peace is not the only illustration we have highlighting this truth. Others, even thousands of years ago, recognized the important role peace needs to play in our daily lives. One such person was Marcus Aurelius, a Stoic and Roman Emperor, who lived between the years of 121 and 17 B.C. He once wrote:

> The first rule is to keep an untroubled spirit. The second is to look things in the face and know them for what they are.[1]

This is exactly what the Lord desires to do in our lives, especially in the beginning stages of His peace process. We first must look to the revealed truth within our own hearts, repent of any lies, and then move forward to receive God's gift of peace within. This important tool is what the Holy Spirit uses to reveal the true matters of our hearts.

We find Jesus discussing the necessity of this weapon of peace in Matthew chapter 10, right as Jesus was instructing His disciples on how to teach and preach in the cities He was sending them to. In the midst of this He suddenly adds something that, at first glance, appears to be in utter contradiction with the principles of Heaven.

He said in verse 34: *Do not think that I came to bring peace on earth. I did not come to bring peace but a sword.*

Luke 12:51 says something similar. *Do you suppose I came to give peace on earth? I tell you, not at all, but rather division.*

What???

Didn't the angels of Heaven declare that the birth of Jesus was bringing peace on earth and goodwill toward men? (See Luke 2:14.) What was Jesus talking about? This just doesn't seem to fit with God's Kingdom of peace. Right?

However, if we look at other verses describing this sword Jesus was referring to, we might be able to get a clearer picture of what He meant.

In the Book of Hebrews, the writer also refers to a sword.

It says:

> *For the Word of God is living and powerful and sharper than any two-edged sword, piercing even to the division of soul and spirit and of joints and marrow, and is a discerner of the thoughts and intents of the heart* (Hebrews 4:12).

In this verse, we see both the words *sword* and *division.* But there is one more place where we see a sword used in the Kingdom of God.

Revelation 1:16 describes the Son of Man standing in the midst of the seven lampstands. John portrays Jesus in this manner:

> *He had in His right hand seven stars, out of His mouth went a sharp two-edged sword, and His countenance was like the sun shining in its strength.*

By putting all these verses together, we now understand the sword Jesus was referring to in the Gospels of Matthew and Luke was the sword coming out of His mouth as He spoke truth to the listeners. This shows us the Word of God acting as a sword that pierces our lives with truth, exposing all that is often hidden inside us.

Hebrews 4:12 describes for us a division between soul and spirit. This would indicate a clear distinction between the works of the flesh and the works of the spirit. No more confusion between the two. We know those who walk in the works of the flesh will not inherit the Kingdom of God, and only those living in the Spirit will successfully walk in the Spirit (see Gal. 5:19-21,25).

While looking further into the words of verse 12, we notice the sword also brings division between *joints* and *marrow.* The use of these two words intrigued me, so of course, I had to look further for the meaning behind them. The definition in the Greek for *joints* is "joint, raised or fitted together,"[2] but this word also makes reference to a chariot and loosening of weights or an anchor.

As I prayed about the significance of *chariot* and *loosening of weights,* I saw a picture of a literal chariot attached to a human with a demon driver cracking his whip, causing the human to be "driven" to the point of absolute exhaustion. While watching this scene, I saw the sword of the Lord come down and divide or separate the human from this demonic attachment.

The word *marrow* refers to "pasture and the act of feeding"[3]; however, the spreading of gangrene is also indicated in this word. In English, we understand the *marrow* as referring to the essential life tissue found within each of our bones.

By combining the truths behind both *joints* and *marrow,* we can see that in one precise slash from the sword of the Lord, the lies we have joined ourselves to and the unhealthy things we might be feeding upon are exposed in our lives. This is not necessary talking about just the foods we eat, but rather the things we might be pouring into our minds from what we are listening to, reading, or watching. This also includes those ungodly thoughts or lies we might be meditating upon.

This sword was not designed for our destruction, but for our freedom!

The Holy Spirit begins His probing and targets the lies of this world, which we have gullibly agreed to, resulting in our own enslavement to demonic forces attempting to destroy us. He brings to our attention the "poisons" that we have been filling our minds with through poor fellowship choices or impure entertainment that eventually acts as gangrene in our systems. If we continue our poisonous feeding habits, we may be forced to make such hard choices as referred to in Matthew 18:8-9.

> *If your hand or foot causes you to sin, cut it off and cast it away from you. It is better for you to enter into life lame or maimed, rather than having two hands or two feet, to be cast into the everlasting fire. And if your eye causes you to sin, pluck it out and cast it from you. It is better for you to enter life with one eye, rather than having two eyes, to be cast into hell fire.*

Now please understand, the Lord was not encouraging us to maim ourselves, but rather He was emphasizing the importance of choices here on earth. If we continue to agree with lies from the enemy or poison ourselves regularly, eventually there will be consequences upon both our minds and our bodies. Jesus is encouraging us to make proper eternal choices rather than easy "normal" choices that may lead to our own spiritual "maiming" or destruction later on down the road.

As the sword of the Lord continues its path directly down the center of our being, we find that not only is He offering us release from the demonically-driven chariot drivers, but He is also allowing us the opportunity to repent so that we might be free from the anchors and weights that so often attach themselves to us.

In continuing with Hebrews 4:12, we see this two-edged sword described as a *"discerner of the thoughts and intents of the heart."* This weapon of peace reveals to us what we are really thinking about even when, by all outward appearances, we are doing all the right things. The search light of the Holy Spirit shines on our innermost intentions when we say or do something, often causing us to cringe at the workings of our flesh interwoven within us.

Verse 13 of that same chapter describes the nakedness we all feel before the holiness of God:

> *And there is no creature hidden from His sight, but all things are naked and open to the eyes of Him to whom we must give account.*

Our natural temptation is to run and hide or try to cover up the things highlighted by this sword of peace, much like Adam and Eve when the Lord called for them in the Garden of Eden after their fall into sin. Though the temptation is natural, we must resist and continue to allow these painful issues to be exposed.

†

The sword of peace skillfully cuts into our innermost being, revealing true thoughts and intentions.

His purpose is to heal, not to destroy. The poisons must be cut out and the medicinal properties of the Word applied. He wants to untie us from the weights that hinder us and clearly expose the lies that have prevented us from moving on in our spiritual maturity process.

Hebrews 12:1 says:

> *Therefore we also, since we are surrounded by so great a cloud of witnesses, let us lay aside every weight, and the sin which so easily ensnares us, and let us run with endurance the race that is set before us.*

The choice is ours.

When we feel the painful cutting of truth running through our hearts, we can choose to harden our hearts and ignore the Holy Spirit's call for *"truth in the inward parts,"* or we can embrace the truth of God's Word and allow our healing from the inside out.

Listen to the words of David as the sword of the Lord was slicing open his heart.

> *Behold, you desire truth in the inward parts, and in the hidden part You make me to know wisdom. Purge me with hyssop, and I shall be clean; wash me, and I shall be whiter than snow. Make me hear joy and gladness, that the bones You have broken may rejoice* (Psalm 51:6-8).

Both Hebrews 3:15 and Psalm 95:7-8 make this appeal: *"Today, if you will hear His voice; do not harden your hearts, as in the rebellion."*

We need the sword of the Lord! We desperately require regular probing into the issues of our hearts. It is the only way to begin this peace process with the Heavenly Father. We must agree with His terms for peace or there will never be any true peace in our lives.

Hebrews 12:11 offer us further words of encouragement to move ahead with this "chastening" process. It says:

> *Now no chastening seems to be joyful for the present, but painful; nevertheless, afterward it yields the peaceable fruit of righteousness to those who have been trained by it.*

To invite the sword of peace into our lives, we might begin by praying Psalm 139:23-24, which says:

> *Search me, O God, and know my heart; try me and know my anxieties: and see if there be any wicked way in me, and lead me into the way everlasting.*

The word *try* in Psalm 139 means to "test, investigate, examine, or prove"[4] the area in question. The word for *anxieties* in the King James Version is actually *thoughts* and refers to our cognition, sentiments, and opinions.[5] This word also speaks of one having a "divided mind." We might think of this in reference to the "double-minded man" in James 1:7-8 who the Bible declares will not receive anything from the Lord because of his lack of faith in the truths of God's Word.

As we pray this verse, we need to tell the Holy Spirit that He is welcome to probe every area of our lives. We are willing to reveal every secret and allow Him to bring the light of truth inside us. As the Holy Spirit speaks, we must be diligent in confessing those areas, asking for forgiveness, and casting out any demonic influence that may have been using those lies to continually bombard us with fears.

When we first ask the Holy Spirit to begin His questioning, we may be tempted to deny or avoid the hard things He brings up. I have found from personal experience that it is pointless to argue with the Holy Spirit in these areas. Quick agreement will help to bring a more rapid resolution to the problem.

Our undisciplined thought patterns have grieved the Holy Spirit numerous times and opened the door to sin in our lives. Now it is time for us to learn the art of capturing and casting down these unruly assassins of truth.

◆ ◆ ◆

Paths of Peace

As we move closer to the Lord's precise piercing of our thoughts and intentions, let us keep in mind that just as a surgeon must sometimes cut into our bodies in order to remove the infection, in the same way, we are the ones who must humbly submit to the full revelation of truth in our inward parts. As painful as the truth may be at times, in order for us to live in peaceful harmony with all of Heaven here on earth, our sin must be exposed.

Ephesians 5:11 urges us to have no fellowship with the unfruitful works of darkness. Just expose and root them out, Paul tells us. This is the only way!

If we will lie still and listen to truth as applied by the speaker of truth, the Holy Spirit, He will begin His accurate surgery of love to set us free from the lies of worry and the cares that have driven us to the point of utter exhaustion. There is a different way to live, a much better and freeing lifestyle that will allow us to experience and remain in this wonderful gift of peace. It's time to press on.

Let's Pray

Lord Jesus, I come before You, humble and broken, even distressed at the number of ways I have allowed fear, worry, and the cares of this life to rob me of the true peace You offer. I know I have allowed my mind to be flooded with poisonous lies, and recognize the ways in which these lies have stolen my joy and peace, which I know are a part of Your Kingdom. Forgive me!

Though I'm not sure what might be exposed, I know that Your sword of truth is necessary in my life, so I ask You to release the sword of peace into my heart and mind so that I can recognize lies, repent of them, and then quickly move to agree with You in all areas. Grant me the courage to lie still and hear all You need to reveal. This is my heart's desire.

Holy Spirit, I'm listening. Speak truth and expose lies, then grant me the grace to receive and embrace Your truths so I can begin feeding on those things which are pure, holy, and pleasing in Your sight. Grant me the grace to continue on Your paths of peace. Amen.

Chapter 3

CAPTURING PRISONERS OF WAR

At times, fear has had a "field day" with my mind. Once old thought patterns were activated, the enemy came rushing in with all the old lies that had previously tormented me. All it took was me agreeing with outward appearances on one point and suddenly sick feelings of fear and panic would set in. This was especially true in the area of finances.

Not long ago, after balancing our checkbook, I happened to go online to check on our current bank account balance. At first glance, our account balance appeared to be nearly the same as a rather large check I had sent off in the mail. Fear instantly assaulted my mind, sending me into an emotional tailspin. I found myself questioning my math in our checkbook and worrying about a recent tithe check I had just given at our church.

The old familiar thought patterns rushed in as my stomach twisted in knots.

"Overdrawn!" I thought. All I could see was accumulating bank fees and more debt.

I was in a panic.

Realizing that the church accountant was working on the deposit that day, I decided to contact her and ask if she could hold our tithe check for a couple of days. After taking care of that, I nervously sat down to rebalance our checkbook.

While reexamining the numbers more carefully, I suddenly realized that the larger check I was concerned about had already cleared. Our checking account balance was fine after all. The fear lifted and welcomed relief set in. I later apologized to the church accountant for all the additional work I had caused her that day.

Yes, it had all been a false alarm; however, what concerned me the most was how quickly the enemy had been able to fill me with panic, causing me to fall back into my old ways. One moment I had been in peace, and the next moment fear had a strangle-hold on me. What had caused my downward spiral in such a short period of time? When I asked the Holy Spirit about this, He responded with one word: *stronghold.*

As I prayed and meditated on this, I realized that I obviously had a stronghold of fear still in place though I had asked for the peace of the Lord numerous times. It was time for that stronghold to be completely dismantled and destroyed forever.

In studying and praying about this matter, I was reminded of Second Timothy 1:7, *"For God has not given us a spirit of fear, but of power and of love and of a sound mind."*

I found that the words *sound mind* refer to disciplined, safe, or sober thinking.[1] If we practice this type of thinking, we would find our passions and opinions becoming moderate and discreet. Part of the definition also includes the word *sozo,* indicating a safe, delivered, and protected way of thinking.[2]

That was exactly what I needed.

In further meditating on Second Timothy 1:7, we can see that the Heavenly Father is not the one giving us thoughts of fear, worry, or anxiety, but He instead has given us the ability to maintain a sound mind through disciplined thought patterns. If this is true, how do we activate this healthy thought pattern in our own lives?

Thinking back to the stronghold of fear highlighted in my own life, Second Corinthians 10:3-5 offers us more information on a stronghold of the mind.

> *For though we walk in the flesh, we do not war according to the flesh. For the weapons of our warfare are not carnal, but mighty in God for the pulling down of strongholds, casting down arguments and every high thing that exalts itself against the knowledge of God bringing every thought into captivity to the obedience of Christ.*

According to these three verses, God has given us the weapons we need to pull down strongholds in our minds. These weapons are not effective if we do battle through our natural human nature or understanding. The purpose for these weapons is the pulling down of strongholds or arguments[3] with God to the actual point of extinction.

Notice the word *arguments* in our verse. The King James Version uses the word *imaginations,* and the definition found in the *Strong's Exhaustive Concordance* speaks of being disputatious about trifles or striving about words.[4] Included in this category of arguments is anything that attempts to capture our attention and hold our focus instead of the Lord Himself (see 2 Cor. 10:5).

†

Mental arguments or excuses often indicate a lie is somehow involved.

These verses instruct us to *cast down* arguments, thoughts, reasoning, or imaginations that prevent us from really knowing God or hearing His voice. This action word describes a violent demolition of the lies desiring to draw us away from the way of peace. Clearly, this is a mental warfare we must learn for ourselves.[5]

Later in verse 5, we see the instruction to bring every thought into captivity, enforcing our mental obedience to the Spirit of the Lord. At first, the mental discipline of capturing every random thought popping into our minds may seem rather challenging for most of us. Our natural tendency is to permit our minds to go wherever they want and to meditate on anything that shows up.

Though we may have the outward discipline to control or monitor our outward behavior, many times our minds have never been subjected to such restrictions. For this reason, the concept of catching every thought and carefully examining it may seem quite daunting at first, but to really enter into the promised peace of the Lord, it is something we must master.

The last portion of Second Corinthians 10:6, at first glance, appears a little brash as it boldly declares *"...and being ready to punish all disobedience when your obedience is fulfilled."* It almost seems as though Paul is encouraging us not to just capture these lies floating around in our heads, but also to "punish" our assailants.

While considering this, I was reminded of how ruthless and persistent the powers of darkness are in their desire to see us fall into eternal destruction. The only recourse we have to "punish" such deviousness is to openly walk in the opposite spirit of what the enemy desired. As justice is carried out, the enemy will see the final destruction of any stronghold they may have built in our lives.

Let's look at more verses to help us further understand the extent of our battle in the area of the mind, our hearts, and our active imaginations. The Lord Himself describes the condition of people's thought lives prior to the global flood in Genesis 6:5, saying that *"...every intent of the thoughts of his* [people's] *heart was only evil continually."* After the flood in Genesis 8:21, the Lord says again, *"...the imagination of man's heart is evil from his youth...."* Later we see the tower of Babel incident where the imaginations of people went wild, causing them to build a tower to the heavens in direct challenge to God their Creator (see Gen. 11:1-9).

The prophet Jeremiah depicts the children of Israel as a rebellious people who would not obey or *"incline their ear"* to the Lord. He says in Jeremiah 7:24 that they *"followed the counsels and dictates of their evil hearts and went backward and not forward."* Later in chapter 9, he indicates that undisciplined thinking was a learned behavior taught to them by their fathers (see Jer. 9:14). First Peter 1:18 also refers to this generational curse as *"aimless conduct received by tradition from your fathers."* The Book of Romans describes a group of people who, although they knew God, refused to glorify God or be thankful toward Him. Here Paul says they became *"futile in their thoughts and their foolish hearts were darkened"* (Rom. 1:21).

Obviously, we can see this battle of the mind is something the whole human race struggles with even from childhood. In order to gain ground in advancing toward spiritual maturity and peace within, we understand that it is absolutely necessary to capture our thoughts. This discipline is something that requires constant awareness. If we can learn to retain thoughts that reflect only the truths of Heaven, we will see the fulfillment of God's great and wonderful promises directed toward us.

Becoming Out of Alignment

Returning to my own mental battle, I agonized over the thought that somehow I still had a mental fortress built up around a series of lies I believed either about God, myself, or others. The worries I struggled with were clear indicators that something was out of alignment with the Kingdom of peace. I desperately wanted to demolish this stronghold of fear, but wasn't exactly sure how to do that.

To begin my healing process, I first asked the Holy Spirit to apply the sword of peace to my heart so everything could be revealed. Next, I asked Him what I needed to do in order to totally destroy the lies I had agreed with in the past. As He walked me through a series of repentance prayers, He then gave me specific instructions on what action steps I needed to take in this area. Once I agreed to His plan, I was able to cast out the spirit of fear and any other tormenters that came in with this stronghold. My final prayer was for the complete and utter destruction of these particular lies in my life. When it was all finished, the peace of God returned.

I was finally free!

Now I must explain that simply because the stronghold had been destroyed in my life did not mean that I could mentally "relax" in this area! No, in fact, in my mental vigilance, I found myself constantly checking to make sure I was not meditating on fear, but instead on the wonderful promises of God. Vocal declarations of God's Word and continual thankfulness kept my mind preoccupied during the first day following my victory. I found not only a flowing peace rushing over my mind, but also increasing joy followed me the longer I remained in His peace.

Francois de La Rochefoucauld, a noted French author of maxims and memoirs who lived from 1613 to 1680, once wrote about peace and tranquility. In his writings, he stated that if we are "unable to find tranquility within ourselves, it is useless to seek it elsewhere."[6] While it is true that eternal peace can never be discovered by looking to the establishment of a "perfect" environment surrounding us, that supernatural tranquility we all desire only comes by making peace with God and allowing His gift of peace to infill us.

Knowing this, it is obvious that mental sin, which leads to fear and a host of other atrocities, clearly opposes the peace of God. Jeremiah 17:9-10 tells us that our hearts are *"desperately wicked"* and have a natural tendency toward sin of all kinds. However, in spite of this, we have a God constantly searching our hearts and testing our minds so He can give each of us *"according to* [our] *ways, according to the fruit of* [our] *doings"* (Jer. 17:10).

The Spirit of God is on the hunt to find individuals who will make the effort to conquer their rebellious thoughts, casting them down and out of their heads. Once our thoughts are filled with truth and we are absolutely convinced of the Father's goodness, we will find ourselves truly overflowing with the rivers of living water (see John 7:38).

Our dear friend, Maria, experienced her own battle against fear as she came face to face with a customs agent while seeking entry into the United States. Maria had already been in our country once just the previous year using a waiver visa, as it is called. Her three-month visit to our church resulted in many amazing friendships and close ties with a number of individuals.

After much prayer, Maria, a native of Germany, decided that she would return once more on a waiver visa and eventually work toward obtaining a Christian worker visa so she could stay for several years as a volunteer to love and serve those God had put in her path. Unfortunately, she made mention of her future desire while going through the customs line. The irritated agent on duty abruptly stopped and began pressing Maria for more details about her visit. The questioning continued as the agent grew increasingly agitated while demanding that she tell the truth.

She was.

The customs agent, after two hours of intense questioning, decided to call me on my phone to confirm or deny Maria's explanation for her visit. My confirmation only seemed to upset him further. Ultimately, the agent decided that everything Maria had said was a lie. Based upon his judgment and that of his equally irritated supervisor, our friend was subjected to another two hours of questioning, and a complete search through every detail of her luggage.

No information was given to her, but she knew that something was going very wrong in her short visit to our state of Washington. Quietly, Maria prayed, asking the Lord to grant her grace for whatever lay ahead. Her concern was not so much for herself, but for those of us waiting to pick her up at the airport and the plans she had made in picking up another friend from the airport herself in the next couple of days.

After four hours, Maria was finally given the opportunity to speak with us while still detained in the customs office. She had finally been told that, because of her comment about desiring to change her visa some time in the future, her entry into the United States had been denied.

She had been deemed "impermissible."

During our brief conversation on the phone, John and I were able to hear what had befallen our friend and were able to pray for the peace of God to cover her. Maria instantly felt a supernatural outpouring of peace and joy encompassing her. Instead of fear and intimidation, she felt compassion and even thankfulness for whatever small comforts the agents offered her while confined to the customs area.

†

Supernatural peace brought her rivers of joy even while surrounded by dark circumstances.

When the agents discovered no more flights would be coming until the following day, they explained to Maria that she would have to be held overnight at the detention center before returning to the customs office the following morning. That was a whole new experience for her!

When it came time for Maria to be moved to the detention center, they explained that she would have to be handcuffed along with several others who were being moved there. Once moved from the airport to the van, Maria was finally able to at least see the city she so longed to visit. Amazingly, she actually giggled as they drove her close to the Tacoma Dome only a few miles from where she had hoped to come.

This is what our dear sister had to say in describing her feelings at that moment.

> I made it to Tacoma after all! As I was spending the night at the North West Detention Center, I couldn't stop giggling when I realized where the officers brought us. I tell you, the Lord was so amazing! I had so much joy and peace throughout the whole time. My joy was a bit disturbing to the officers, both at the customs office and now at the detention center as well. One of the officers actually commented saying, "Gosh, you are the cheeriest inmate I have ever seen!" I know it was not me, but Christ smiling in me was smiling back at them. Thank you, Lord!

While in the holding tank awaiting her turn to be processed (it literally took all night!), Maria was able to minister to a young Chinese woman who was being deported back to China. Depression was all over Xiog, but she expressed how much it helped her to have Maria by her side. While Xiog spoke of her willingness to sacrifice things in order to find happiness in life, our German sister explained how Jesus had already paid the sacrifice for our eternal happiness.

Later in the evening, Maria found herself with two Guatemalan ladies, illegal aliens, who were to be deported back home. Though finding some difficulty in communicating, she did discover that both ladies were Christians. During the long night spent in yellow scrubs given her by the detention center staff, her new friends were able to teach Maria praise songs in Spanish which they took great joy in singing loudly, filling the facility with echoes of worship as the presence of God permeated the room.

Finally early the next morning, though exhausted from lack of sleep, Maria was picked up from the detention center, handcuffed once more, and returned to the customs office. With no place to lie down, Maria ended up lying directly on the cold floor just to find some type of relief from the fatigue that enveloped her at times.

We were permitted one more phone conversation with her during which we assured her everything was taken care of on this end and we would work with her on getting the correct visa so she could return soon to our country. Gratefully, Maria thanked us for our help. That same evening, our exhausted friend flew back home to Germany without any further incident.

Through her long hours of confinement, Maria discovered how even with imprisonment one can experience a supernatural sense of freedom within. She now says this experience totally opened up her heart and understanding to how Paul and Silas could be singing while imprisoned as described in Acts 16:24-25.

> *Having received such a charge, he* [the jailer] *put them into the inner prison and fastened their feet in the stocks. But at midnight Paul and Silas were praying and singing hymns to God, and the prisoners were listening to them.*

The joy of the Lord and the peace of God are two things that cannot be taken away from us regardless of our circumstances. The overflowing of living waters flowed freely even though Maria was behind bars for a time. This type of test revealed to our sister that she did indeed carry everything she needed to overcome the thoughts of fear and despair that might have otherwise set in.

In all our circumstances, we need to remember the intense love of our Father from our earliest conception in the womb as described for us in Psalm 139. His passionate gaze upon us follows us from our greatest heights to our lowest pits. There is not one detail about us that He is not already aware of. The purpose of His constant examination, however, is not for our destruction, but instead for our deliverance from lies so we can experience His truth.

The sacrifice of Jesus has prepared a means of escape from our mental and physical prisons in the same manner Maria experienced it. The way of peace has been placed before us. To attain this supernatural peace, we first must conquer our unruly thoughts and imaginations so we can truly experience the thoughts and mind of Christ in an unhindered fashion (see 1 Cor. 2:16).

What an amazing gift we have been given!

Let us declare in agreement with the words found in Second Peter 3:14, *"Therefore, beloved, looking forward to these things, be diligent to be found by Him in peace, without spot and blameless."*

Paths of Peace

I know the temptation for many of us is to just ignore this portion in establishing a mind that is set in peace because it seems like way too much work. After talking with many of my brothers and sisters in the Lord, I am convinced that the area of mental disciplines for many Christians is rarely discussed or taught. Many of us figure that if we look spiritual on the outside, all is well. Unfortunately, that is not how the Lord evaluates us. He is not impressed by outward behavior at all, but instead is consumed with what is happening in our inward parts (see Ps. 51:6).

The Lord knows that if we are convinced of what is true and holy, that knowledge will naturally shine through us and cause us to be transformed outwardly as well. This is why a checklist of good behavior will never bring about a renewed mind! We must saturate our minds with the truth in order for us to become fully persuaded.

Fortunately, the Lord understands our weakness and though He does not condone our sin, He has offered us an incredible Helper who can cause us to become victorious in any area we ask for His assistance in. He is called the Holy Spirit. If we ask, the Holy Spirit will answer. That is God's promise!

Let's Pray

Lord, I come before You in open transparency in regards to my mind. I admit that I have allowed my thoughts to wander as they will, accepting nearly any lie the enemy chooses to place there. For this, I ask for Your forgiveness. I no longer want to permit the establishing of mental strongholds by agreeing with lies.

I choose You! I choose Your ways of truth! I choose to walk on Your paths of peace so I can be in agreement with all of Heaven. I receive Your gift of forgiveness and declare that my sin no longer exists. It has been washed away through the precious shed blood of Jesus Christ.

As I have now been forgiven, I speak to you devil and declare your past work in the area of my mind is now null and void. By the power of the Holy Spirit, I destroy every stronghold and lie that you have fed me! I do not believe what you say because you only speak lies! I silence your voice right now and command you and any other demon associated with lies in my mind to leave me now! I send you to the feet of Jesus!

Holy Spirit, I now ask that You come and flood my mind with Your gift of peace. I desire to be filled with the goodness of God and renewed joy. Grant me the strength and wisdom to guard this gift of peace by carefully examining every thought to see if it is in agreement with Heaven or not.

Thank you, Lord for setting me free! Amen.

Chapter 4

SHOD YOUR FEET

One evening, my husband and I found ourselves sitting in front of the television with our young grandson, Gilead, watching the movie *Hook* starring Robin Williams and Dustin Hoffman. Though it is only a newly revised children's story, both John and I saw captured within this colorful tale a parallel to our daily battle for peace.

This film depicts a grown-up Peter Pan with a wife, children, and a flourishing career as a lawyer. With his adopted name of Peter Banning, this work-obsessed man finds himself forced to return to "Never Land" when his old rival, Captain Hook, kidnaps Peter's two children and challenges Peter to a showdown.

Much has changed for Peter. The realities of his legalistic world have all but erased his memories of Never Land, the lost boys, and most especially his ability to fly. Without the gift of flight, he would never be able to defeat Captain Hook and rescue his children.

The real battle for Peter begins when he recognizes his own mind is preventing him from believing his true identity as Peter Pan and from accessing what he needed to begin flying once again. Though desperate for this change, his transformation did not take place until he could discover his "happy thought," the birth of his firstborn son. Once Peter realized where true happiness was found, his real identity and ability to fly were restored, ultimately bringing about the release of his children and the defeat of Captain Hook.

In applying the principles of this adventure tale to a real-life scenario, we understand that it takes much more than just a "happy thought" for us to experience a complete mental and spiritual transformation in the Kingdom of God. However, if we were to look at Peter's "happy thought" as representing the peace of God, we can see some similarities.

Once we find the peace of God flowing through our minds, we must work to keep that peace by carefully guarding our thoughts and teaching ourselves to only meditate on the good, true, pure, and holy things spoken of in Philippians 4:8. By being in agreement with the Kingdom of peace, we will begin to see changes and transformations taking place in our lives and in the lives of others around us.

When our hearts have been completely filled with the peace of God, we are then commanded to "shod our feet" in preparation for walking out in peace before the world around us. Ephesians 6:15 says, *"having shod your feet with the preparation of the gospel of peace."*

The word *shod* indicates a type of shoe or sandal bound tightly around our feet enabling us to walk through rough or difficult places with our peace firmly intact.[1] In that same verse, *preparation* describes well-adjusted individuals who have made all the necessary changes to their thought patterns.[2] This strong internal fitness allows them to move out and be successful in spiritual exploits as directed by the Holy Spirit.

So what does it look like for one to have feet properly shod? Isaiah 52:7 explains it in this fashion.

> *How beautiful upon the mountains are the feet of him who brings good news, who proclaims peace, who brings glad tidings of good things, who proclaims salvation, who says to Zion, "Your God reigns!"*

In essence, the Spirit of the Lord is saying that it is a beautiful thing to see His children walking with their feet tightly bound in peace as they boldly proclaim the things they are clearly hearing from the Father. This *beauty* is further described as being at home or in unity with the Kingdom of peace.[3] Matthew 5:9 refers to these greatly blessed peacemakers or peaceable ones as sons of God.

†

Beautiful feet indicates our minds have become completely convinced and saturated with His peace.

In contrast to this Kingdom of peace, we are told that wherever envy and self-seeking exist, we will find confusion and *"every evil thing"* (see James 3:16). First Corinthians 14:33 confirms this by informing us that God is not the author of confusion. However, found within the safe boundaries of God's wisdom or a heavenly mindset, in addition to peace, we will also discover true purity, gentleness, a willingness to yield, a merciful heart, and good fruit blossoming from our lives with a total lack of hypocrisy (see James 3:16-17).

Verse 18 in James chapter 3 clearly states that in order for us to see the fruit of righteousness, the work of the Kingdom must be *"sown in peace by those who make peace."* In other words, we must not only have God's peace mentally locked in place, we also need to learn how to pass this peace on to others in order for our work in the Kingdom to produce lasting fruit.

What Are We Afraid of?

George MacDonald, a Scottish author, poet, and Christian minister who lived from 1824 to 1905, described something he called a "sane, wholesome, and practical working faith." He said:

> It is a man's business to do the will of God; second, that God Himself takes on the care of that man; and third, that therefore that man ought never to be afraid of anything.[4]

Often, surrounded by today's society, we can become convinced that it is absolutely natural and normal to have overwhelming fears. Many feel that the only way out of fear and stress is to go to Heaven, leaving this fallen world. Though that might be true in one sense, it is definitely not God's intention for us to just put up with the fears, but rather to overcome them!

As I look back in my own life, I can remember times when I could literally feel the peace of God covering me, allowing me to receive that which the Lord desired for me to have. One particular occasion involved the healing of my right arm.

Shortly after my husband John and I were married, our band called "In Season" decided to travel up north from our California homes to minister in churches along the west coast. Excitedly, the two of us, my brother, Charles, and our friends, Joe and Steve, took some time off from our jobs just prior to the beginning of summer so we could begin our year-long ministry journey. One of our first stops happened to be in the small town of Port Orchard, Washington, where my sister and her family resided.

With a free day before our scheduled evening services, we ended up playing badminton in my sister's backyard. The weather was perfect, and we all enjoyed the exercise and challenge that came with batting the plastic birdie back over the net to each other.

The game progressed along with points accumulating for each of the teams. However, at one point I moved back just a little too far to hit the birdie. As boundaries for the game, we had placed small spindly logs collected from the forest surrounding the property. When my foot stepped on the log behind me, it rolled, causing both my feet to fly out from underneath me.

Instinctively, my hand went back behind me to try and stop my fall. The weight of my entire body was suddenly inflicted upon one arm. Within a very short amount of time, my entire right arm swelled up to nearly twice its normal size and turned an ugly shade of purple.

We knew we were in trouble!

With no insurance and limited cash for our journey, a visit to the doctor seemed impossible, so we prayed. The arm did not improve. Fortunately, I was only a vocalist and did not have to play any instruments so we could continue with our scheduled concerts for the time being with my pitifully swollen arm in a sling. Our only option was to wait and see what God would do.

It was nearly a week later before we arrived at a church that insisted on sending me to the doctor so we could find out exactly what had happened during my fall. Once at the hospital, I was ushered into the examination room where the doctor very soberly examined my now multi-colored arm.

He cleared his throat and began questioning me regarding my profession.

"Right now, I'm singing and traveling with our Christian band," I explained.

"Well, if you were a professional tennis player, I would suggest surgery for your arm," he stated. "However, since you are not using your arm in that way, I think we can just let it heal itself."

I was a bit relieved for the moment, but then he continued with his analysis. He explained that when I fell, tremendous pressure was exerted on my right hand, causing the tendons in my arm to tear up near my elbow.

"Are you right-handed?" he asked.

"Yes. Why?"

"Well, when your arm heals, it will not be as strong as it was previously. In fact, you will probably find that your left arm will be stronger and will have to compensate for that."

The bad news continued.

"And as far as your right arm is concerned, you will never be able to fully straighten it out again. The way it is right now is the way it will be from now on."

I was shocked! Peering at my slightly bent limb, I couldn't believe that he was telling me the damage was permanent. This is not what I had envisioned for my future, especially as we had only been married a few months!

Tears welled up in my eyes. I was still in shock at the news as I came out to my awaiting husband. All I could do was cry in his arms. It was more than I could handle! We quickly left the emergency room and returned to our friends, bearing the bad news.

A couple of days after the doctor's verdict, we were invited to lead the worship at a Full Gospel Businessmen's Fellowship gathering. After our music, the guest speaker got up and shared an amazing testimony of healing he experienced some years ago. Listening to the incredible things God had done in his life boosted my faith, so my husband and I went forward at the end to see if this man would pray for us.

He prayed, but nothing happened. My arm still appeared the same as it had previously. While we were walking away a bit disappointed, another gentlemen approached us asking if we had received the healing we were hoping for.

We told him "no." Well, could he have an opportunity to pray for us as well, he asked? Both of us were a bit skeptical about this "normal" guy praying for us. The man of faith had just prayed and nothing had happened, but realizing that it couldn't hurt, we agreed.

As this man prayed, I noticed something different about him. There was a sense of peace as he began speaking to my arm to be healed. John sensed something as well, so he encouraged me to try straightening out my arm. Before I even had a chance to think about it, John gave my elbow a slight push upward. The arm completely straightened out without any sensation of pain!

From that day forward, my arm has been completely normal. My right arm is not weaker than my left as proclaimed by the doctor, and I still favor my right hand as always. Praise God!

The man who prayed for me was a man of peace. We could sense it in his gentle demeanor. He was led by peace to pray for me; thus his prayers were sown in peace. His peace and confidence in the Lord brought about lasting fruit of righteousness in my life exactly as described in James 3:18. The peace of the Holy Spirit just naturally drew us into faith to receive the gift of healing the Lord desired to give us.

Feet Wrapped in Peace

Returning to our reflections upon beautiful feet tightly bound in peace, we see in John 14:23 where the Lord promises to make His continuous abode with those remaining in agreement with His Gospel of peace. It says, *"If anyone loves Me, he will keep My word and my Father will love him and We will come to him and make Our home with him."*

When we abide or remain in His peace, the Holy Spirit is able to cover us in peace, lead us out in peace, and pour peace upon others through our lives. However, even when abiding in peace, there will still be times when the Lord and others may need to "wash our feet" in the Spirit to help remove any remaining residue from the world to make certain we are in all readiness for our "adventures in peace."

Jesus Himself initiated this necessary foot-washing just prior to the last supper when He humbled Himself before the apostles and began washing the residue of the world off of His followers. We're told in John 13:9-10 that at first Peter resisted Jesus, but once Jesus explained the necessity of the washing, Peter requested that Jesus not only wash His feet, but also his head and his hands. Jesus responded saying that he had already been "bathed" by the words of peace they heard spoken by Jesus (see John 15:3; Eph. 5:26). Peter and the others were only in need of a foot-washing so they could be completely clean.

†

Regular "foot-washing" with the Word removes the dusty residue we pick up from this world.

While meditating on this, I saw a picture of sandaled feet dusty from the dirt path the person was walking upon. This traveler only needed to have his feet washed in order to be freed from the dust collected upon each foot. While traveling on this earth, it is inevitable that we will become "dirty" at times from the ways of the world—but our minds are not completely polluted. We just need to do a quick cleansing of our thoughts by allowing the purity of God's Word to freely wash over us. Once this has been done, we will find our feet once again tightly shod in peace.

Isaiah 55:12 tells us that once our minds have been locked in agreement with the peace of God, we will then go out with joy and be led out with peace. The mountains and the hills around us will respond by breaking into singing, and the trees will joyfully clap their hands in witness to these sons and daughters of peace.

Though I'm not exactly certain what singing mountains and clapping trees would look like in the natural world, I do know that Romans 8:19-22 describes all of creation eagerly awaiting the full revelation of the sons and daughters of God. These are ones who will fearlessly walk in the Kingdom of peace and boldly declare the peace of God over all that is around them.

It says:

> *For the earnest expectation of the creation eagerly waits for the revealing of the sons of God. For the creation was subjected to futility, not willingly, but because of Him who subjected it in hope; because the creation itself also will be delivered from the bondage of corruption into the glorious liberty of the children of God* (Romans 8:19-21).

What a day we all have to look forward to!

◆ ◆ ◆

Paths of Peace

The concept of going after strong mental disciplines in order to be properly shod with the shoes of peace may seem somewhat foreign to many of us who have been Christians for a number of years, but the Word of God is very clear on this. We must have the peace of God tightly wrapped around us before we can truly deposit the peace of God into the lives of others. Only those things sown in peace will bring back the peaceful fruit of righteousness we all desire.

If we consider the washing of our feet by noting the example of Jesus, it seems that others must be involved in this process. Often we don't notice the dirt on our feet when coming in from outside, but one who is taking care of the house will notice immediately. The dirt must be washed off first before we can enter the abode, and then our shoes of peace must be put on before beginning our journey.

The washing of feet by someone else is a very humbling process as they take your dirty foot, look at it, and then in gentleness begin to wash off the dirt so you may freely roam about the house. When we are in need of a spiritual "check up," often the Holy Spirit will send someone who, knowingly or unknowingly, will speak truth to our spirits. If we are willing to humble ourselves, repent, and receive the truth, our feet will be cleaned.

Let's Pray

Dear Lord Jesus,

How many times have I rushed out the door, eager to work within Your Kingdom, but have neglected to first have my feet washed in the Spirit and then reapply the shoes of peace? Often my tendency is to just press on and not take the time to examine my thoughts to see if they are still in peace. When You have sent others to wash my feet with truth, do I ignore the very things You desire to pour into me? Forgive me, Lord!

My heart's desire is to allow others to wash my feet and to tightly wrap the shoes of peace on so I will only be led by peace and become a person of peace so Your work of righteousness can effectively flow through my hands to others. Wash me now in the fountain of Your peace so I can see Your seed of truth flourish both in my life and in the lives of others I have contact with. Let me truly become the child of God that all of creation is longing to see manifest here on earth!

Thank you, Lord, for Your amazing gift of peace! Amen.

Chapter 5

THE SENTINEL OF PEACE

The discomforts of pregnancy had set in, and Kristi found herself struggling to even take a normal breath at times. Moments of panic hit as she fought to get air into her lungs. Eventually the "attack" subsided and she was able to relax for a time until the next bout with breathing issues occurred. Both she and her husband assumed that this was a normal experience caused by the anxiety of a first birth and that her symptoms would soon go away.

They did not.

Days after the birth of their son, they both noticed "weird stuff" showing up. Kristi would panic easily, especially when their son cried. The thought of caring for the infant alone frightened her. She would cry non-stop for hours, and when the sun set, she experienced feelings of terror.

A visit to the doctor labeled her experiences as "postpartum blues," but these symptoms continued long after they should have receded. Pills helping her to relax were all the medical field could offer her, but she was reluctant to go that way.

Finally, in desperation, Kristi cried out in prayer asking the Lord to deliver her from the "black hole" she felt herself in. The following morning when she awoke, mercifully she found some of the symptoms had vanished. After counseling with their pastors, Kristi and her husband realized that most of what she had experienced was a spiritual attack and it was up to them to shut any open doors of sin in order for the lies of insanity, anxiety, terror, and fear to leave.

Through prayer and godly instruction, Kristi was taught how to battle any attempted attacks in the future. She learned the importance of keeping her thoughts in check. Any time she noticed fear or anxiety attempting to flood her mind, she had to stand up and battle by resisting those thoughts and then immediately going into praise and worship before the Lord.

"In the beginning, it was hard," Kristi admitted. "It took me a few days to get used to recognizing those thoughts as soon as they came. I had to work hard to keep them from swimming in my head, but once I understood what to watch for, the thoughts began to come less frequently. My confidence in the Lord and His authority totally increased through all this."

The importance of examining our thoughts is once again highlighted in Kristi's testimony. She learned how to carefully guard the doorways of her mind by literally scanning every thought before permitting it to "swim in her head."

Her faithfulness and diligence in learning to battle for peace brought the release she needed from this tormenting attack. The peace of mind Kristi attained made a huge difference both in her life and in the lives of her family.

Paul the apostle describes this same type of mental vigilance in Philippians 4:6-7 where he instructs us:

> *Be anxious for nothing, but in everything by prayer and supplication, with thanksgiving, let your requests be made known to God and the peace of God, which passes all understanding, will guard your hearts and minds through Christ Jesus.*

The word *guard* is crucial as it indicates that God's peace will act as "watcher in advance," keeping careful attention to everything that tries to enter our minds.[1] The definition of *guard* also offers us a picture of spies or a sentinel being posted at the gates of a city. Anything looking suspicious is carefully examined before entering.

Our part is to make that choice in agreement with peace. We must forbid worry or anxiety into our minds by remaining in a constant state of prayer and spontaneous thanksgiving for all God has done and is doing on our behalf. By meditating on the goodness of God and the many promises He has offered those who are in agreement with the Kingdom of peace, we will assure that there literally will be no room for fear to enter.

If God's peace lifts, we need to train ourselves to stop and examine our hearts at that moment. What thoughts have we allowed in? What are the meditations of our hearts at that moment? What actions are we involved with?

†

Lifted peace offers advanced warning when something is out of alignment with Heaven.

Once we have located the culprit, we must be quick to repent and then drive out the invader. When fear has been removed, we then can fill our minds with the truths God has given us. Sometimes declaring these truths aloud is helpful in establishing the peace of God back into our hearts.

Another verse describing this same process is found in Colossians 3:15 where Paul says, *"And let the peace of God rule in your hearts, to which you were called in one body; and be thankful."*

This verse clearly demonstrates our necessary cooperation in this whole process. We must allow the peace of God the privilege of governing or ruling in our hearts. We must decide what we are allowing to "swim in our heads" at any given moment. If we want peace, then we must train ourselves to listen to the Holy Spirit as His peace rules and governs over our hearts.

It's interesting to note that in these last two verses, we see an emphasis on thanksgiving as an important tool triggering the release of peace in our hearts. Again, if our minds are filled with the praises of God, there really is no place for fear to lodge itself.

Jerry W. McCant, professor of New Testament Greek in the Department of Philosophy and Religion at Point Loma Nazarene College in San Diego, is quoted as saying, "In a world filled with causes for worry and anxiety…we need the peace of God standing guard over our hearts and our minds."[2] To fully engage this gift of peace, we must diligently seek to keep our minds lined up and filled up with the truth. If we don't, there are plenty of worries that would love to take over and flood us with fear.

In order to maintain the peace of God in our minds, my husband and I have adopted a simple rule to follow. We have said, "No peace, no go." In other words, if the peace lifts, we stop and ask the Holy Spirit for His direction at that moment.

We find Jesus using this peace to calm the hearts and minds of those He was ministering to. In Luke 7:50 Jesus spoke words of comfort to Mary after she washed His feet with her hair. Jesus said, *"Your faith has saved you. Go in peace."*

In another incident, when the woman with the issue of blood was healed, Jesus again spoke to the woman's heart. *"Daughter, be of good cheer. Your faith has made you well. Go in peace"* (Luke 8:48).

Both of these broken women needed to have the peace of God released into their tormented minds. Fear was driven out as a part of their healing, and in its place Jesus proclaimed His peace.

The word used for this peace is *eirene,* meaning "a joining together with His peace, prosperity, quietness, rest, set at one again, calmness, an absence of strife, and tranquility."[3] Doesn't that sound like something we all want in our lives?

So often we are trained and taught by those around us to worry and fret over many areas of our lives. We see others striving and running after the things the world waves in front of us like bait. Once fear has worked its way into our lives, we can actually become accustomed to functioning in fear and stress as a normal part of our day. This, however, is not the way of peace Jesus proclaimed over those women.

I believe this *eirene* peace is a part of our heritage as followers of Jesus. This amazing gift of peace is available if we are willing to do the battle necessary to hang on to it. We must learn to lean on the voice of peace as it whispers warning and direction for us moment by moment. A forewarning from the Sentinel of Peace can prevent much pain and sorrow. If we listen, we can respond and follow His wise counsel.

I am convinced that when we arrive in Heaven, we will be astonished at the number of times "something" caused us to change our minds about going a certain direction or traveling at a planned time. Though we may not recognize it at the time, this was the work of the Sentinel, a voice I want to become far more familiar with in the days ahead.

Once that peace has been established in our lives, it can become an integral part of who we are. One can actually live without worry, anxiety, and strife if peace is permitted to reside and rule in our hearts. If we choose the paths of peace, we are promised a journey here on earth that is full of joys and pleasures that only come from the Kingdom of peace.

Paths of Peace

Learning to take our place as watchmen on the walls of our minds is something that we must teach ourselves to do constantly. It is our job to guard over the mental assaults the enemy loves to throw at us. A lack of attentiveness to this area will result in increased attacks, worry, and fears about nearly everything. If the enemy sees he can get away with these mental assaults in one area, he will often attempt new areas as well until he has us locked down in fear, as we saw in Kristi's case mentioned earlier in this chapter.

The Sentinel of Peace wants to stand guard over our minds. He wants to warn us long before the enemy breaks in to steal, kill, and destroy. His purpose in our lives is to warn us in advance of the attack by causing the peace of God to lift. By learning to listen, we can be forewarned and avoid the schemes of the enemy. How valuable could this be?

To attain this *eirene* peace, we must confess and lay down our fears so we can mentally join ourselves with the peace of Heaven. Even if we don't feel the peace of Heaven at first, if we ask the Holy Spirit to lead and guide us into prayers of repentance over lies we have agreed with, the Lord will not hold back any of His good gifts.

"Ask and you shall receive," Jesus says. "Seek and you will find. Knock and the door will be opened to you." (See Matthew 7:8.)

All we need to do is make the exchange. We give up the lies, and He will replace them with His peace.

Let's Pray

Dear Holy Spirit,

I ask You to scan the thoughts and intentions of my mind right now to see if there are yet any lies of the enemy that I have agreed with. Highlight those lies before me, so I can be quick to repent. (Whatever lies He shows you, repent for agreeing with those lies.) Thank you, Holy Spirit, for continuing to search my heart and mind for anything that does not agree with the peace of Heaven.

Right now I destroy any strongholds of the enemy in these highlighted areas that may be present, and I invite the eirene *peace of God to cover and fill every portion of my mind.*

Now, Holy Spirit, I ask that You teach me how

to listen to Your voice and pay attention to the peace that is now residing within me. I choose to be diligent and mindful of this peace in the days ahead.

Thank You for the Sentinel of Peace.

Chapter 6

TAKING GROUND

The birth of our third son appeared to be perfectly normal at first. Regular contractions began indicating it was time for us to leave for the hospital in anticipation of his birth. We were taken to a birthing room where John patiently waited by my side, encouraging me to breathe each time the muscles contracted. My sister, Cathy, a nurse by profession, was also there with me for much of the process.

Sometime during the morning, we noticed a change in the expression of the nurses as they checked the fetal monitor attached to our baby still in the womb. Each time I had a contraction, his heartbeat stopped briefly. My sister came in to see if the monitor was connected properly.

It was.

By this time, John could tell something was going wrong and stepped out to call our pastor for prayer support. While he was gone, things seemed to move at a whirlwind pace. Doctors, nurses, and hospital staff were all rushing around me. The baby was in stress, and they determined an emergency C-section was needed.

Because the contractions were coming every couple of minutes at that point in my labor, there was no hesitation on my part when they asked for permission to do a C-section. I was ready for this baby to be born. Within minutes, I was prepped and moved from the labor room into surgery. John wasn't even present for the final decision because he was still in the hallway talking with our pastor!

In surgery, the staff moved quickly to put me out so the baby could be delivered. I still remember the anesthesiologist telling me that I would only feel one more contraction before falling asleep. What a relief!

In the meantime, poor John was still out in the hallway, literally pacing back and forth with concern. Once the baby was delivered, the nurse wrapped our son in a blanket and rushed from surgery toward the infant intensive care unit down the hall. As she brushed by John, she simply informed him he had a son and without further explanation, entered the unit. Fortunately, one of the pastors from our church arrived and was able to pray with John as he battled thoughts of fear, both for me and our new son.

Once our son was settled under a heat lamp with sensors running from his chest and an intravenous tube attached to the top of his head, John was allowed to come in and examine our 6 pound, 11 ounce baby with his little chest rising and falling in his struggle to breathe normally. His irregular heartbeat was clearly displayed on the monitor. A holy boldness came over John as he announced to the staff that he was going to pray for our son. Gently, he laid his hands upon our baby and prayed with all his might.

It was hours before the grogginess of the anesthesia finally wore off. John was right there as I awoke. The baby was the first thing on my mind.

"How is he?" I asked.

"He's in intensive care, but doing OK right now," John explained. "The doctors say he has an irregular heartbeat they are concerned about."

"Can I see him?" That is when the nurse intervened.

"No, not yet. You just came out of major surgery. You need time to recover."

That was not what I wanted to hear.

Everything within me desired to see this child I had carried for nine months. With the general anesthesia I had been given prior to surgery, it hardly felt as though I had actually given birth. Soon my recovery was sufficient enough for me to be moved into a regular hospital room. Without a newborn by my side, the room felt cold and empty. Seeing other women with their newborns only brought tears to my eyes.

I wanted to see my son!

A couple of hours later, I finally convinced the nurse to take me down to the intensive care unit. Though warned that it might be too soon for me to move around, I was placed in a wheelchair while still attached to an IV and slowly pushed down the hallway toward the intensive care unit. I had only arrived at the doorway when my head started spinning. All I could see was blackness. Quickly, the nurse pulled out some smelling salts to bring me back to consciousness.

The following day I was finally able to visit my tiny son with sensors and wires running from various places all over his body. We could see his little chest heaving with every breath. The heart monitor still showed an irregular heartbeat as he lay in the warm incubator. None of that mattered. All I could see was a beautiful little boy whom I knew was a gift from the Lord to us.

"When can I hold him?" I asked, while carefully studying all his little features.

"Not yet," I was told. We had to wait until the IV could be moved to his foot, allowing easier movement from the incubator. By the third day we were finally able to hold our precious son. Even with my own body still recovering from surgery, I insisted on feeding our son myself each time he was hungry. Though moving back and forth between my room and the intensive care unit down the hall was a bit difficult, the exercise actually helped speed up my own recovery.

Soon after our son's birth, the doctor came into my room, explaining some of his health concerns. During labor, the baby was in some kind of stress and had a bowel movement while still in the womb. His irregular breathing and heartbeat indicated that he may have swallowed or breathed in some of the contaminated fluid. Apparently, this can sometimes be fatal to newborns.

As the doctor explained the seriousness of the baby's condition, I listened politely, but something else had arisen in my heart—absolute peace and confidence that the Lord intended for our son to live and not die. When the doctor finished, I acknowledged everything he said, but my response was resolute.

He would be fine.

I could tell the physician was a bit put off by my lack of concern regarding our son's symptoms. He felt I was simply in denial so others were sent to my room in an attempt to convince me of the seriousness in this matter. Even a friend from church who was a medical doctor came in to speak with me. Though I understood what they were telling me, the Holy Spirit had planted that gift of faith within my heart and that could not be shaken.

After five long days of standing in this confidence, the medical report finally came back. Our son was finally given a clean bill of health, released from intensive care, and allowed to go home.

The Lord had answered my faithful confidence in His promises.

Even before fully understanding all the Holy Spirit was leading me in, somehow I instinctively found that in my moment of greatest need, from my inner person I was able to pull out a gift of confidence in the promises of God. This gift was merely a fruit of truths I had faithfully filled my mind with while studying and applying the Word of God in my life.

Isaiah 32:17-18 describes for us just what the true work of righteousness in our lives will accomplish. It says:

> *The work of righteousness will be peace and the effect of righteousness; quietness and assurance forever. My people will dwell in a peaceful habitation, in secure dwellings, and in quiet resting places.*

The word *work* indicates action or a transaction that takes place between the believer and Spirit of God operating within us.[1] This spiritual work of agreeing with God and all He speaks helps to dislodge the lies that we have been born and raised with. Every time a lie is dislodged in our minds, the lie is exchanged with truth and an increasing peace with God.

This transaction will eventually lead us to a quiet assurance or confidence in the goodness of God. If we continue in this work of righteousness in our lives, we will eventually find ourselves literally dwelling in peaceful habitations, secure dwellings, and quiet resting places regardless of what type of circumstances we find ourselves surrounded by in the natural.

†

A positive spiritual transaction occurs each time we exchange a lie for the truth.

Just as the rebirth of our spirit is a spiritual transaction that occurs at the moment of our salvation, in the same manner this stronghold of supernatural peace is also established by disciplining both our minds and tongues to move totally in agreement with the peace of Heaven. The Holy Spirit sees this as a spiritual transaction. Once we begin seeing and understanding this Kingdom of peace, we will find total peace as we recognize our true spiritual reality!

When the enemy realizes that we have stood our ground in maintaining the peace of God, he soon recognizes his attacks of fear are futile in this newly established stronghold. The stronghold of God can become a "safe place" where we can rest from all our self-motivated labors, allowing the Spirit of God to lead us only where the Father desires us to go. The more we discipline our minds, the more areas of established peace will be maintained in our lives.

Peace Is An Established Place of Being

The reflections of Henry Miller may add a bit of clarity to our study here. An American novelist and painter who lived from 1891 to 1980, he once said, "If there is to be any peace, it will come through being, not having."[2] How true this is! The kind of peace we are examining here cannot be found in the compiling of wealth, obtaining of fame, or pursuit of power. Peace comes only when we are in alignment with God, permitting His peace to become a literal stronghold within our minds.

To grasp the concept of mental strongholds of peace, we only need to look in Old Testament accounts of Israel finally entering the Promised Land to obtain their inheritance. In Deuteronomy 11:24 and in Joshua 1:3 we find the Lord speaking to both Moses and Joshua about the method in which the children of Israel were to possess the land. They were told not just to enter the land, but to tread upon the land.

The word *tread* infers walking upon something, causing it to bend. It also tells us to string our bow and be observant in the process.[3] Psalm 91:13 also uses the word *tread* and describes us treading upon the lion and the cobra. The lion is a picture of the "roaring" of lies we must face down in our paths,[4] while the cobra represents the twisting of truth the enemy specializes in.[5]

In order to begin taking ground against our enemy of fear, we first must learn how to ignore the threats of our "giants" and recognize the twisting of the truth when we hear it. Our confidence must solely be based upon the truth that is firmly engrafted into our hearts. This is what we move upon and nothing else!

The children of Israel were instructed not to just come in and attempt taking over all the Promised Land at once. They were told to take possession of it bit by bit, one battle at a time. This same principle is true in our own lives. As the twisted lies or fears are revealed to us, our job is to trample down those lies or fears and then richly apply the truth of God's Word to those areas. I have found that by declaring those truths repeatedly and studying the deeper meaning they carry, I eventually become absolutely convinced in both my mind and heart so that God's truth prevails over any lies of the enemy.

In walking through this process, I am treading upon the lies of the enemy and establishing God's stronghold in my own life. A stronghold, in the positive sense, is a mental place of absolute confidence in the truths of God, as mentioned in Psalm 91:1-2.

> *He who dwells in the secret place of the Most High shall abide und the shadow of the Almighty. I will say of the Lord, "He is my refuge and my fortress; my God, in Him I will trust."*

Once one stronghold of faith has been set up, I am in position to begin going after the next tormenting lie in my life. Each established stronghold of peace brings with it an increased amount of God's peace flowing in me and through me.

In any given moment throughout the myriad of life experiences we face, we are always given the opportunity to look only with our natural eyes and respond in fear or to look out from our stronghold of peace and be at rest, even during the most trying of situations. The question I always ask myself is this: Who do I really believe to be the final authority in every situation? If my confidence is in God and the goodness He promises, how can I possibly be afraid of anything?

From my vantage point, safely within God's stronghold of peace, I can be absolutely convinced that all things are in my Father's hands. The Holy Spirit will guide my steps and guard my mind with His gift of peace!

◆ ◆ ◆

Paths of Peace

How daunting it must have been for the children of Israel to be told they were to tread upon the land in order to obtain it as their inheritance! We know that the first generation to come out of slavery could not imagine coming against the giants of the land God had promised them. Because they did not believe the words of God, that faithless generation died in the wilderness, unable to obtain that which God had given them as an inheritance. The following generation of Israelites was next called upon to come and take that which was theirs according to the decree of their Creator. Though it belonged to them, they had to be willing to fight and possess their promises.

This is the same call that each of us has been given.

Though peace is part of our amazing inheritance, we are the ones who choose to either fight and receive or withdraw in defeat. All power and authority to conquer the lies of worry and anxiety have been made available to us, but we must teach ourselves to adhere to the truth so we can effectively conquer the mental lies the enemy throws at us.

The Father in Heaven is eagerly watching our development as sons and daughters of God. He is waiting to see if we will accept our rightful position of authority on this earth and begin treading down every fearful lie before us. He is thrilled to see each time we establish a mental stronghold of peace so we can prepare for our next feat of faith.

The choice is entirely ours.

Will we become champions of faith, or will we spend the rest of our time here on earth wandering around in the wilderness of fear?

Let's Pray

Dear Lord Jesus,

More than anything, I desire to become one of Your champions of faith! I want to tear down and demolish strongholds of fear, replacing them instead with strongholds of peace. I know that this is entirely possible and that You are yearning to see me become all that You have created me to be, so I ask for all the strength and determination it requires to conquer every mental fear I battle.

You have created me to become an overcomer here on earth, and I declare that I have all the mental abilities to identify and destroy those lies that have hindered me in the past. Thank you for making the areas of my weakness Your strength. I declare that I am strong in You! (See Joel 3:10.) Your Word is true and in this I have peace!

I humbly ask for Your forgiveness in believing any lies about my mental weakness. I know You have already given me everything I need to conquer the lies of fear. Please wash me now in Your cleansing blood. I receive Your wonderful gift of forgiveness. Thank You.

Right now I speak to every voice that tries to tell me I am weak and unable to establish strongholds of peace in my life. I declare that you are all liars! The Spirit of God within me has made me strong against you. You are defeated! I command you and every other spirit that came in as a result of this lie regarding my weakness to all join hands and go from me. I don't want you any more! I destroy your stronghold in the mighty name of Jesus and send you to the feet of Jesus!

Holy Spirit, I ask You to come and fill me once again with even more of Your peace. Flood every area with Your presence so I can establish strongholds of peace in my own life. Thank You for making me more than a conqueror in the area of peace. Amen.

Chapter 7

PEACE OR PASSIVITY?

While volunteering at our church's community services outreach, my husband and I have the opportunity to observe firsthand the extreme results of those either unaware of the truth or those often unwilling to put out the necessary effort to conquer the lies of the enemy running rampant in their own minds. The consequence is a vicious cycle of constant need and an unhealthy dependency upon government and church handouts.

One person in particular comes to mind as I think of the great destructiveness of giving passivity free reign. Ron[1] at one time had both a family and a productive job, but when things went sour for him, his response was to drink, allowing the alcohol to numb his emotions. Eventually alcoholism took over and Ron soon found himself jobless, homeless, and abandoned by his family.

Literally living in city parks with other camps of homeless individuals, Ron began to spiral downward even further; a drunken stupor was more prevalent than sober moments. In this state, he somehow stumbled into our community services where trained counselors convinced him that Jesus had a much greater purpose than spending his days drunken and hiding under a bridge somewhere.

Yes, Ron surrendered his life to Jesus, and things immediately began to turn around for him. The drinking stopped, most of the time. He was able to move in with another Christian brother for a season and then was blessed with his own fully-furnished apartment, thanks to a federal program designed to help former war veterans.

His cabinets were filled with food. He had a working phone line and people could get in contact with him. He was even able to get cable television set up in his cozy apartment. The regular disability checks and food stamps he received would be able to get him through each month quite comfortably, but much was still lacking in his "new" life.

Though the physical surroundings had changed for Ron, his mind still ran in the same damaging cycles of lies that had taken him down in the first place. This mental recycling kept Ron weak and unstable. His double-minded ways would allow him to agree with Christians desiring to pray for him, but his unwillingness to discipline his thoughts kept him from truly receiving the fullness of all God had for him (see James 1:8).

Even in this greatly improved living situation, Ron was often tempted to go back to his old crowd of friends and return to his old ways. Many times, he would spend all his finances on foolish or destructive things that left him once again dependent upon the Christian friends trying to assist him in making this change.

What was the root of the difficulties Ron was facing? Passivity. Ron was unwilling to make the additional effort needed to fight the lies of the enemy, but instead allowed his mind to remain in "neutral" while filling his time with television entertainment and other mental distractions. He chose this rather than working to fill his mind with the life-changing seeds of truth found in the Word of God. Feelings of weakness and helplessness hit any time temptations of the enemy flooded his mind. At times, he would just give in to the thoughts and then often found himself acting upon these temptations. His continued passivity led to additional feelings of guilt, hopelessness, and self-pity.

Just as Ron had his struggles with passivity, we find examples of this type of difficulty and the generational consequences portrayed in the life of Eli, the high priest described in First Samuel 1–8. We are told that Eli, a man who once honored and feared God, began a downward spiral as he made choices based on his pride[2] and personal comfort (see 1 Sam. 2:25).

The first mention of Eli is found in First Samuel 1:9 where we see him sitting near the tabernacle of the Lord observing Hannah as she pours out her heartfelt anguish to the Lord in regards to her barrenness. Though she was very sincere and passionate in prayer, we find Eli wrongly judging this woman with accusations of drunkenness (see Judg. 1:13). Much to Hannah's credit, rather than taking offense to his harsh words, she humbly explained herself and Eli blessed her request (see 1 Sam. 1:17).

Though Eli's lack of discernment in accessing Hannah's situation is a bit disturbing, his continued path of passivity begins to reveal even more serious consequences. In First Samuel 2:12 we're told that the sons of Eli were corrupt and did not know the Lord. Just by examining this simple statement, we can understand a lot about Eli and his lifestyle.

As a part of God's chosen people, the children of Israel were exhorted over and over about the importance of instilling the truths of God's Word into the lives of their descendents (see Deut. 6:5-9). However, more importantly, the descendants of Levi were given charge over the tabernacle of the Lord and their need to know and be passionate for the things of God was even more evident (see Num. 1:49-53).

It is obvious from the earlier description of Eli's sons that this high priest had somehow neglected to train up his sons in any kind of reverence or fear of God. Their great spiritual lack was demonstrated by both the meaning of their names and their behavior.

The name of Hophni[3] means "a fighter," while Phineas[4] means "the mouth of a serpent." We find these feisty and deceptive young men terrorizing the children of Israel by having their servants forcibly take the best cuts of raw meat from those making offerings in the temple rather than waiting until the fat was cut off and burned and the raw meat boiled, as was customary (see Lev. 3:3-5). This threatening and greedy behavior of both Hophni and Phineas caused the other tribes to resent bringing in their offerings to the temple (see 1 Sam. 2:17). In addition, we also find Hophni and Phineas committing fornication and adultery with the women who worked around the temple (see 1 Sam. 2:22). We know that Phineas was married while committing these crimes (see 1 Sam. 4:19).

What was Eli's response to all these reports of blatant sin coming to him in regards to his sons?

In First Samuel 2:23-25 we see Eli scolding his sons for their behavior, but his words fell on deaf ears. Deuteronomy 21:18-21 gives very clear instructions on how rebellious children were to be taken outside the city and stoned, something Eli was very aware of. However, Eli's response to these reports was still in line with what he had done all along: nothing!

†

Spiritual passivity leads us down a dangerous path with grave consequences affecting many.

As Eli continued in his passivity, we see the consequences growing more and more intense. At this point we see an unidentified man of God coming to him and warning of the things that were to come (see 1 Sam. 2:27-36). The man of God informs Eli that in his passivity, he literally despised the offerings given to God by honoring the will of his sons more than God. First Samuel 2:29 tells us that Eli even partook of these fatty cuts of stolen meat from his sons, causing him to become fat in his gluttony. His love of the easy and comfortable way not only resulted in the premature death of his sons, but also a lack of spiritual power and authority (see 1 Sam. 2:31), spiritual blindness and great grief (see 1 Sam. 2:32), generational poverty, and the eventual removal of all of his descendants as priests in the temple (see 1 Sam. 2:36).

In First Samuel 3:11-14, young Samuel repeats the same words of coming destruction, but in this prophetic word, we are given further insight into Eli's response to the sins of his sons. Verse 13 tells us that, though he observed the vile sins of his sons, he did not restrain them. Through Samuel, Eli hears that his passivity had gotten to the point where there was literally no offering or sacrifice that could atone for this sin *forever* (see 1 Sam. 3:14). Eli repeatedly chose to esteem his sons and their ways more than God Himself. Matthew 10:37 offers us the New Testament version of this warning. *"He who loves father or mother more than Me is not worthy of Me. And he who loves son or daughter more than Me is not worthy of Me."*

Proverbs 22:6 adds to our understanding of how Eli failed his sons by not following through with all we are commanded to do in the raising of children. *"Train up a child in the way he should go, and when he is old he will not depart from it."*

The word *train* means "to narrow, to initiate or discipline."[5] This indicates that, as parents, it is our responsibility to be the initiator of clear boundaries for our children and their behavior. The training of our children must also include godly discipline for times when those boundaries are crossed. Admittedly, this training does require a lot of effort on our part, but after looking at the severe consequences Eli suffered for his passive ways, we can see that spiritual vigilance on behalf of our descendants is a much preferred way!

While following the "domino effect" of one man's passivity, we see in First Samuel 4 that though the word of the Lord was flowing through Samuel, Israel was gravely affected by the lack of spiritual discernment in their high priest and his sons. When they attempted to go to battle against the Philistines, they were defeated. In desperation, the elders of Israel decided that what they needed was a more physical presence of their living God, so they called for the Ark of the Covenant.

With spiritual blindness running rampant, the ark was taken to battle, the Philistines still defeated Israel, the ark was captured, and Hophni and Phineas were killed. At the news of this disaster, Eli fell back, broke his neck, and died (see 1 Sam. 4:18). Phineas' wife, upon hearing the news, gave premature birth to a son whom she didn't even care about (see 1 Sam. 4:20) and named him Ichabod,[6] saying "the glory has departed" before dying. I'm sure poor little Ichabod had to deal with some major rejection issues while growing up! Talk about a sad ending!

Unfortunately, there are yet other long-range consequences to Eli's passivity as well. Not only were the direct descendents of Eli affected, but also those around him were impacted. Some negative influences can be observed in Samuel's life as we take note of his parenting skills in the years that followed.

We are told that though Samuel was an eyewitness to the terrible devastation inflicted upon Eli, his family, and Israel as a nation, there were some obvious "learning gaps" this young man experienced just by being around such blatant passivity. Though Samuel was a godly prophet who continued faithfully in serving Israel, somehow his love and devotion for the Lord was not adequately passed down to his own sons.

In First Samuel 8:1 we are told that Samuel's two sons, Joel and Abijah, were made judges over Israel. The good news is that Samuel learned not to place an early curse upon his children by naming them things such as "fighter" and "mouth of a serpent." Joel means "Jehovah is his God"[7] and Abijah means "father, worshipper of Jah."[8] Unfortunately, Samuel's early years spent around Eli's passivity may have caused him to still be a bit passive himself in the spiritual training of his sons.

We find in First Samuel 8:3-5 that Samuel's sons *"did not walk in his ways,"* but instead turned aside to dishonest gain and the taking of bribes, and by this they perverted justice in the land of Israel. Sadly, the behavior of these boys caused all of Israel to call for a king rather than continuing with the practice of having judges rule over the land.

This turn of events came as no surprise to God, however. We are told in Genesis 49:10 that God already had a plan in place for one righteous and final king to come through the tribe of Judah: Jesus. For this we all can be eternally grateful!

†

We can choose to accompany God in His battle for our peace.

Though Eli and others have struggled with the effects of passivity, many others have been successful in their call to action. One such man is Eivind Josef Berggav (1884-1959), a much-celebrated Norwegian Lutheran bishop known as Primate of the Church of Norway. He once commented that peace was won by accompanying God into battle.[9]

This man of action has been recognized for his leadership in the Church of Norway's resistance to the Nazi occupation of Norway during World War II. Though isolated and under house arrest during much of the war, this man of God inspired the people of Norway to actively resist the lies of Nazism.

In the same manner, we are called to act in obedience to the voice of the Holy Spirit when he alerts us to lies trying to infiltrate our minds. By resisting fears, the Holy Spirit will give us all we need to defeat the lies of the enemy and cast him down.

The New Testament also speaks very strongly against passivity. James 1:21-25 calls each one of us to act upon our faith and beliefs. It says:

> *Therefore lay aside all filthiness and the overflow of wickedness, and receive with meekness the implanted word, which is able to save your souls. But be doers of the word, and not hearers only,*

> *deceiving yourselves. For if anyone is a hearer of the word and not a doer, he is like a man observing his natural face in a mirror; for he observes himself, goes away, and immediately forgets what kind of man he was. But he who looks into the perfect law of liberty and continues in it, and is not a forgetful hearer but a doer of the work, this one will be blessed in what he does.*

As we've read in previous chapters, in order to become "doers" of the Word, we must take a number of action steps. First, we are instructed to deliberately lay aside all vile, shameful, and disobedient acts that would cause us to be hardened or unreceptive to the implanting of truth in our hearts. Once those things are laid aside, we humbly come before God asking that He literally engraft His truth within our hearts so that our souls can be transformed and made whole.

†

An effective "doer" conquers every fear or lie the moment it attempts to infiltrate.

The next action James encourages us to take is one of acting upon the truths we've been given. Becoming a *doer* of the word means being one who, like a poet or performer, is able to take words written on a page and bring them to life.[10]

To be a *hearer* only means being one who continually hears undeniable truths flowing into his mind, but quickly allows mental arguments and reasoning to rob him of the obvious so he can maintain his "happy" state of delusion[11] before the truth has the opportunity to take root (see James 1:23-24).

In contrast, the doer looks into the mirror and continues looking, allowing the Word of God to take root in his heart. Once he is fully convinced of the truth, he is able to walk out those truths in his life as empowered by the Holy Spirit.

Looking or gazing at the truth includes an indicated action of bending beside and peering intensely into[12] so that the one examining the truth will finally be able to understand the truth from a position of liberty, as a citizen rather than a slave.[13] From this standpoint of truth, we are transformed from glory to glory.

Sadly, we can only wish that Eli had emerged out of his comfortable lifestyle and aggressively worked to train his sons in the knowledge of God. Had he actively and obediently continued his own passionate pursuit of the Lord, we might have seen a totally different outcome in his life and the lives of many generations to follow.

Now the question remains: How many of us have fallen into the trap of passivity, allowing our personal comfort levels to dictate the lives we now live?

The Lord's call to us is one that requires diligent mental effort to keep our minds locked in agreement with Heaven. It is our agreement with the convicting power of the Holy Spirit that allows us to be healed and delivered from tormenting lies so we can press forward in our spiritual maturity within the Kingdom of God.

◆ ◆ ◆

Paths of Peace

Dreams and fantasies of "the good life" often fill our minds, especially as we feed upon false images presented by current media. The main goal for so many seems to be the pursuit of comfort in every avenue of life; yet the Bible tells us in Matthew 13:22 that it is the cares of this world and the deceitfulness of riches that will choke out the growth of God's truth in our lives, causing us to become unfruitful. This is exactly what we saw occur in the life of Eli, the priest. His love for the "easy way" resulted in death and destruction in his life and in the lives of his sons.

Quite a heavy price to pay for passivity!

In contrast to this false type of peace, we find the Word of God exhorting us to diligently keep our hearts (or minds). We see this in Proverbs 4:23 which says, *"Keep your heart with all diligence, for out of it spring the issues of life."*

This verse tells us we need to diligently guard and watch over the thoughts and meditations of our minds, testing to see whether we are in agreement with the thoughts of Heaven. We do this because the fruit of our thoughts will be reflected within our lives on this earth.[14] If we become absolutely convinced of the truths of God's promises to His sons and daughters within our minds, we will begin living and walking in the same love, peace, power, and authority of Jesus.

This is what we all desire!

Let's Pray

Dear Lord Jesus,

I come before You in complete humbleness asking for Your forgiveness for every way I have walked in passivity rather than in diligence. Forgive me for allowing my love of comfort or "the easy way" to dictate how I respond to You and the things You have called me to do. I understand this to be sin. Please forgive me! I no longer want to walk in passivity.

I do not want to see the fruit of passivity in my life or in the lives of future generations in my family line. I ask that You wash me clean in the blood of Jesus and sever any generational sins that may be passed down to my children. I declare that my children and descendents will be blessed and not cursed, in Jesus' name.

Now I speak to you passivity and any other spirit that may have come in as a result of my passivity. I tell you now that you all must leave me immediately! I destroy any foothold that you may have had in me and declare that you cannot come back! Your work in me is finished!

Holy Spirit, I invite You to come and flood every part of me with Your true peace so I can begin to understand what it means to maintain Your gift of peace within. I specifically ask for Your strength and diligence to begin actively walking the paths of peace rather than the laziness of passivity. Teach me how to attentively guard my heart and mind so I can be in complete harmony with all of Heaven.

Thank You for hearing and answering my prayers. Amen.

Chapter 8

SET AT ONE AGAIN

A dear friend, Lydia[1] came over one morning to have a time of prayer. She was feeling completely burned out from all the interpersonal ministry and felt as though she had no more energy to press forward. Her discouragement was apparent. It was all over her face.

As we sat down to chat, she began revealing all the worries and concerns for both her family and friends that were literally devouring her joy. Hearing her amazing testimony for the first time, I was in awe of all the Lord had already accomplished in her life.

Before her entrance into the Kingdom of God, Lydia had dabbled in Tarot cards and even learned how to read them for herself. She was eager to know the truth and thought that the secrets she desired could be found by consulting the powers of darkness. Her life continued in its downward spiral. Thinking she might need some help in understanding the cards, she went to a medium.

As a part of their time of consultation, Lydia was instructed to mediate for a time so she could "better connect" with the powers. During her time of mediation, Lydia suddenly found herself on a beach where she could see a bright light approaching her. She knew this light was the Lord, so she turned to move in the opposite direction.

Instantly, two very large and fearsome-looking warrior angels grabbed her arms, forcing her to look toward the light. They sat her down on a log with them on either side and she watched as this light grew to the size of the sun. The ocean in front of her suddenly became as clear as glass as the light from the Son of God touched the edge of the water.

When she awoke from her trance-like state, she angrily grabbed her belongings and left. She had not anticipated an encounter with Jesus and was upset that this could happen during her meeting with a medium!

It was some time later when she and her husband, out of desperation, decided to attend a class offered at a church to help with their fragile marriage. During a prayer time following one of the sessions, a gentle-spirited woman on the team was suddenly given a picture of Lydia sitting on a log at the beach with two big angels sitting beside her. She described the whole scene exactly as Lydia had seen it!

Lydia finally understood how the love of Jesus had been pursuing her even before she knew Him. As all resistance melted away in the incredible love of Jesus, both Lydia and her husband surrendered their lives to Jesus that day.

It had been some years since that first encounter, and through the busyness of church and family activities, somehow Lydia now found herself weighed down with life. As we prayed that day, I spoke the peace of Jesus over her before proceeding in our "spiritual housecleaning." The more we invited a greater infilling of the Holy Spirit, the more she noticed she was having a physical reaction to His presence.

The Holy Spirit was quick to identify the source of both her heaviness and physical reaction so she repented of lies she had agreed with and asked the Lord for forgiveness; then we were able to quickly drive the enemy out. As tears streamed down her face, I again asked for fresh infilling of both the love and the peace of Jesus to be upon her.

†

Lies caused both heaviness and a physical reaction to the presence of God's peace.

As the peace washed over her, the weariness retreated. A new stirring began moving within as rivers of joy began gushing up from her innermost being. Together we rejoiced in seeing a literal fulfillment of Jesus' declaration:

> *If anyone thirsts, let him come to Me and drink.*
> *He who believes in Me, as the Scripture has said,*

> *out of his heart will flow rivers of living water* (John 7:37-38).

It was an amazing morning!

Later, her husband came up to my husband reporting that he felt as though he had a brand-new wife! Her joy and uplifted countenance caused her face to beam with the overflow of God's love. The change in her was remarkable, and I rejoiced in God's remarkable weapon of peace, which He had enabled me to use.

Some might wonder just how peace is actually a powerful weapon in God's Kingdom of peace. In an earlier chapter we spoke of the sword of peace, which represents the "cutting" power of the Word of God. Its truth will literally lay us open before God so the Holy Spirit can test and probe the thoughts and intents of our hearts.

The first time I spoke peace over Lydia's heart, the sword of peace was applied, bringing every lie and scheme of the enemy to the surface. Once those things were dealt with, I once again spoke the peace of Jesus over her so her heart could be set at one again with the Kingdom of Heaven.

We see this same kind of scenario played out for us in Luke chapter 7. Jesus is dining with Simon the Pharisee when a woman with the reputation of a "sinner" entered the room (see Luke 7:36-39). The broken woman came in with her precious alabaster flask of fragrant oils and stood weeping behind Jesus. It's obvious that the sword of peace had already penetrated her innermost being. The thoughts and intentions of her heart had been laid bare before Jesus without a word being uttered.

Her tears fell upon His dusty feet.

In a passionate display of true repentance, the woman began drying Jesus' feet with her hair, kissed His feet, and then broke open the flask pouring out the costly treasure upon the man who had touched her heart with His great compassion. No judgment came out of this lover of humanity, only love and empathy for the life she had lived.

Bristling with religious pride and arrogance, Simon looked on with disgust as the woman massaged the oils into Jesus' feet.

"If He truly was a prophet, he would never allow such a vile creature to touch Him!" Simon thought.

Hearing the thoughts bombarding Simon's mind, Jesus asked him to consider the parable of two debtors. One owed 500 denarii and the other 50.

"If both debtors were forgiven their debts by the same creditor," He asked him, "Which one would love him more?"

"I suppose the one whom he forgave more," he replied.

Then Jesus made reference to all the woman had done since entering his house. Her brokenness was undisputable; her repentance, undeniable; her great love, unmistakable.

The sword of peace had accomplished its purpose. Now it was time for her to be set at one again.

Jesus turned to the repentant woman and declared her sins forgiven. Her great debt had been cleared. The others began mumbling among themselves.

"Who has the authority to forgive sins?" they whispered to each other. Ignoring their questions, Jesus continued with His "peace process."

"Your faith has saved you," He declared over the teary-eyed woman. "Go in peace."

Can you imagine her joy and ecstasy in realizing that all the horrible details of her past life were immediately erased? She didn't have to walk about covered in guilt and shame any longer! She was given a new start in life without the burdens of her past. Wow!

Do you remember how as children we would often make a mistake while playing a game and ask for a chance to do it over again? Now as adults, how many of us would love to have the opportunity for a "do-over" in our lives? How much would we sacrifice if we could erase every ugly mistake we've ever made?

The amazing truth is that we ***have*** been given this opportunity through the gift of true repentance. There is nothing we have ever done that cannot be covered by the blood sacrifice Jesus made on our behalves! The only thing we need to do is actually believe and receive His forgiveness so all of our past debts and mistakes of our lives can be completely erased from our hearts.

What a gift Jesus has given us!

Now in taking a closer look at the words Jesus spoke over this precious woman, once her sins had been forgiven, we see Jesus declaring that her faith had saved her. The word *faith* speaks of persuasion or conviction in the truthfulness of Jesus' words,[2] bringing her the wholeness or salvation she sought. In essence, her absolute belief in the words of Jesus was able to completely transform her mind so that she no longer felt the guilt and shame that had hung over her for many years. She was free!

The next instruction given her was, "Go in peace." Jesus tells her that she is free to be on her way, only this time she leaves liberated from her "death sentence" and enveloped in *eirene* peace, which allows her and her Creator to be "set at one again."[3] She now can experience the love and peace that comes with our spiritual connection to the Kingdom of God, and Jesus has just completed another "rescue mission" for one of the lost lambs.

In her world, all is well. A new day has arisen!

Simon, the Pharisee and all his friends saw a living demonstration of how deep the love of the Father goes when confronted with a truly repentant heart. Even before the blood of Jesus was shed for our many sins, this "reject" of Jewish society was able to experience a new life and the gift of peace because she willingly bore all her guilt and shame before Jesus.

Though drawn by the life and testimony of Jesus, one would need to compare Simon and his friends' responses to that of the older brother in the well-known story of the prodigal son in Luke 15:11-32. The older brother was unable to rejoice at the restoration of his "worthless" brother who had wasted his portion of the inheritance.

What is astounding is that neither Jesus nor His Father considers any person worthless or beyond repair no matter what state they find themselves in. The only key to receiving God's gift of a "do-over" is genuine humility and repentance before God. If we are willing to let go of the lies from the enemy and truly believe all that Jesus says about us, then we are next in line to receive our miracle of redemption!

†

The onward progression of peace is accomplished by conquering one mental battle at a time.

When contrasting God's gift of *eirene* peace to the long and difficult road people often trudge upon when attempting to establish their own forms of peace, the differences are apparent. John F. Kennedy, (1917-1963) the 35th President of the United States, once made this observation about his own peace efforts:

> Peace is a daily, a weekly, a monthly process, gradually changing opinions, slowly eroding old barriers, quietly building new structures.

> And however undramatic the pursuit of peace,
> the pursuit must go on.[4]

In contrast to President Kennedy's slow and often fruitless efforts in attempting to establish peace, we find the Bible full of examples memorializing those who experienced amazing and immediate changes as the peace of God enveloped them. One such story is found in Mark 5:25-34 where a desperate woman had an issue of blood that plagued her body for 12 long years. All her money had been spent in search of a medical solution through the hands of physicians, and nothing had succeeded. Her condition only grew worse.

However, we're told that this dear woman had convinced herself that Jesus did carry the healing power of Heaven within Him and that in acknowledging or agreeing with the truth of His words, she could receive her healing. She recalled prophecies of the coming Messiah found in Malachi 4:2 which said:

> *But to you who fear My name the Sun of Righteousness shall arise with healing in His wings; and you shall go out and grow fat like stall-fed calves.*

If only I could even touch His clothes, she thought to herself, *I will be made well* (see Mark 5:28).

In complete confidence in the promises of God, she did touch His clothes and received her gift of physical healing. As we saw in the earlier story of the woman washing Jesus' feet, Jesus also instructed this woman to "go in peace." However, because of the physical nature of her ailment, He said one more thing. He added, *"...and be healed of your affliction"* (Mark 5:34).

The word *affliction,* or *plague* in the King James Version, reveals the demonic nature of her physical sufferings as it refers to a whipping or scourging similar to the Roman flagellum used for criminals.[5] The sole purpose of her disease was to cause her as much suffering as possible. Knowing that, Jesus not only spoke internal peace over this dear woman, but then addressed the afflicting spirit as well, declaring that all the damage he had previously caused was now *sozo*, or "healed."[6]

As we read further in this chapter, we see Jesus continuing His errand of mercy on behalf of the ruler of the synagogue (see Mark 5:35-36). Just as the woman had been healed and sent off in peace, the servant arrived with heart-rending news. The ruler's daughter had already died.

Look carefully at Jesus' instructions to this devastated father. Seeing his anguish, Jesus tells him, *"Do not be afraid."* His fears or phobia[7] came into direct conflict with the Kingdom of peace the Lord was trying to establish in this man's heart. *"...Only believe,"* Jesus continues. In other words, Jesus instructed him not to allow these words of doom to rob him of the faith and confidence he had previously placed in Jesus.

It's like Jesus is saying, "Engage your heart in the Kingdom of peace and keep your focus on my words of life, not on this negative report." To help guard this man's fragile faith, Jesus only allowed Peter, James, and John to accompany Him as they walked toward the ruler's home.

We know the end of this story.

After driving out all the grieving doomsayers from their home, Jesus went into the little girl's bedroom, took her by the hand, and commanded the ruler's daughter to rise up. The 12-year-old not only rose up, but also began walking around, demonstrating her complete healing and restoration, a natural result of walking in alignment with the Kingdom of peace (see Mark 5:37-43).

By examining the application of peace in the life of my friend, Lydia, the woman washing Jesus' feet, the woman with the issue of blood, and the ruler of the synagogue, we can begin understanding the importance of learning to have our hearts knit together with Heaven's covering of peace. In casting down all our fears and embracing the truths pouring through the voice of the Holy Spirit, we can not only be "set at one again" ourselves, but also begin bolstering up the fragile faith of others so they too can be walking in agreement with Heaven.

I love the words of Jesus as He describes the importance of us seeking His conditions of peace. Using the language of a parable, Jesus says in Luke 14:31-33:

> *Or what king, going to make war against another king, does not sit down first and consider whether he is able with ten thousand to meet him who*

> *comes against him with twenty thousand? Or else, while the other is still a great way off, he sends a delegation and asks conditions of peace. So likewise, whoever of you does not forsake all that he has cannot be My disciple.*

The Holy Spirit is sounding out the call even now. The war between light and darkness has been ongoing since the fall of Adam. However, we understand that darkness cannot and will not win. The enemy has already been defeated!

†

Jesus called him to engage his heart in truth rather than focus on natural circumstances.

The armies of God will come upon this earth (see Rev. 19:14), and by that time, it will be too late to make peace with the Kingdom of Heaven. The offer for conditions of peace must take place in each of our lives before our time is up. To make peace with the Prince, His stipulations are simple. We surrender everything—all the lies, all the sin, all our failings—and He will take our old fallen nature and replace it with one that is overflowing with love, peace, and joy.

Sounds like a reasonable exchange to me!

◆ ◆ ◆

Paths of Peace

While still considering the vivid pictures portrayed for us in the accounts mentioned in this chapter, we can only wonder how many times we may have missed hearing the voice of the Holy Spirit as He worked to establish a heart of both confidence and peace within us.

"The healing is yours," He might have whispered. "If only you would be fully convinced of that in your mind! Then you, too, could not only receive your healing, but also walk away covered in His gift of peace."

Though some of us have been exposed to the healing power of God moving through us at different times, how many of us have heard the words, "Go in peace"? The Lord desires us to not only be healed, but to also be at one again with the Kingdom of peace. His hope is to see us absolutely covered in peace so the enemy will not be able to quickly assault us again.

Peace is our covering. Peace removes all sense of past failures and allows us to begin again with renewed strength and reenergized hope. Peace is that which literally transports us from the clutches of fear into the arms of our loving Father. Peace indicates that we are fully convinced of the promises of God within our minds.

Peace is a good place to be!

I am convinced that if a former prostitute and a deathly ill woman were able to be healed and walk away in total peace that we can as well. When we see a desperate father holding on to the words of Jesus in spite of the report he heard from his servant, then we can also have that same kind of conviction for our own lives.

If we will work to guard our thoughts and only embrace the things that Jesus says, we can partake of His gift of supernatural peace resting upon a supernatural life! It's ours for the taking!

Let's Pray

Dear Lord Jesus,

I look upon the accounts of these real people who, in spite of their histories, were able to receive forgiveness, healing, and even resurrection life as their inheritance simply because they fully believed the things You said and responded to Your call for faith. Once they were convinced, they received. They were able to walk away in total harmony with the Kingdom of Peace. They were set at one again.

This is what I want!

I want to be fully convinced in my mind of Your goodness and mercy that You desire to pour out upon me. I desire to hunger after You with all my being. Let my thirst for You increase with every new day. Above all, I cry out to see my mind set at ease as I learn to live and move and have my being fully settled into Your gift of peace.

I no longer want to listen to the lies of the enemy. Forgive me for agreeing with the lies of the enemy in the area of peace. Wash me now in Your blood so I can be healed of all that ails me, both physically and spiritually. I receive Your forgiveness now.

In the name of Jesus, I come against you spirits of doubt and unbelief that desire to rob me of the many gifts my Father has in reserve for me! You have been defeated by the sacrifice of Jesus! I destroy your work in my mind and body. You have lost your ground, and I no longer want you in my life. I command you and any other spirit that came in with you to join hands and all leave me now! I send you to the feet of Jesus! Go!

Holy Spirit, I know You are my comforter, one who desires above all to see me led by peace and guarded by peace. Today I choose to yield to You so You can speak to my heart and flood me with truth. Fill every part of me with new faith, hope, and most especially the peace of Jesus.

Thank You for teaching me how to treasure this amazing gift of peace. In Jesus' name I pray this. Amen.

Chapter 9

SPEAK PEACE

One Saturday afternoon while ministering to a group of people in regards to acquiring their inheritance in the Lord, the Holy Spirit instructed me to pray for individuals who were experiencing physical pain in specific areas of their bodies. A number of people responded, so I began praying and we witnessed a number of instant healings as I moved down the line.

Several months later, when I returned for a visit to this church, an elderly woman approached me. She wanted to tell me what had happened after I laid hands on her and prayed.

Prior to our prayer time, this woman had suffered greatly in the area of stress and worry. She worried about everything! Not a day went by that she did not experience some kind of stress in her daily life. So great was the weight of stress upon her that she found it difficult to drive or go anywhere in her car.

Aware that this was not what God intended for her, she took a huge step of faith by enrolling for a school of the supernatural offered by a local church. By surrounding herself with people of faith, she hoped that all her fears would be eliminated.

They were not.

In fact, even while attending the various classes held on different nights and days of the week, this sweet little lady began to notice that her body was beginning to react negatively to all the fears she constantly carried about with her. The left side of her face began to sag. Searing pains ran down her face, through her neck, and all the way to her upper back.

This is when I first encountered her at the church.

As I laid hands on her face, neck, and back, I commanded all fear to go and then spoke the peace of the Lord all over her. Right after I prayed, she knew something had happened. All the pain lifted and she immediately experienced the peace of God flooding her body.

†

The declaration of peace brought instant healing and deliverance from worry and stress.

By the end of the session, she knew she needed to drive home, but this time when she got into her car, things were very different. She suddenly noticed that all stress and worry had lifted off her, and that dear saint was able to drive home in perfect peace for the first time in many years! She later noticed that even the left side of her face was no longer sagging!

Even several months after receiving her healing and the gift of peace, she informed me that she has had no reoccurrence of any of the physical pain or symptoms she had previously experienced and now is able to drive wherever she needs to go in complete peace.

Isn't God amazing?

On another occasion, a young man we'll call Daniel came to us completely broken and desperate for a change in his life. Though he had received prayer prior to this, he had finally come to the end of himself. Together we went before the Lord asking for some keys to unlock the cycle of anger, frustration, and stress he was experiencing, often on a daily basis.

Almost immediately, we heard several lies that had been bothering Daniel for a number of years. Once identified, he was able to pray through by repenting and casting out those specific spirits attached to the lies. As soon as this was finished, we invited the Holy Spirit to flood him with peace.

He promptly noticed a change, but what was most encouraging was the report that came nearly a month later. Daniel reported that he could feel an increasing sense of peace dominating his life. Instead of the intense striving for spiritual accomplishments or performance, Daniel now noticed he was able to rest in the fact that God would do whatever needed to be done in his life within His own timetable. With the pressure gone, he found the peace of God easily settled over him.

Eleanor Roosevelt (1884-1962), First Lady of the United States from 1933 to 1945, once offered her opinion on humanity's constant pursuit of peace. She said, "It isn't enough to talk about peace. One must believe in it. And it isn't enough to believe in it. One must work at it."[1]

As true as Eleanor's observation might be, we have come to understand that the only work that brings about lasting peace is that which is sown in peace by those who have made peace with the Creator. As we discover God's paths of peace, we then can witness fruitful works through our own lives by speaking peace over others as seen in the previous two testimonies.

We can see another example where peace is verbally spoken over the backslider in Isaiah 57:19-21. It says:

> *I create the fruit of the lips: Peace, peace to him who is far off and to him who is near, says the Lord, and I will heal him. But the wicked are like the troubled sea, when it cannot rest, whose waters cast up mire and dirt. There is no peace, says my God, for the wicked.*

When considering a life void of peace, the prophet Isaiah quotes the Lord as saying that life is like a choppy sea where the filth and contamination are swirling around in polluted waters. However, we see the Spirit of God calling out to all who will listen; "Peace, peace!" He says. The good fruit coming from our lips will speak His words of peace to those who are far off (the Gentiles), and to those who are near (the Jews).

The Lord's heart is for peace!

His passion and desire for Israel is once again described in Isaiah 27:5-6, where the Lord describes Israel as a vineyard. He makes His plea for peace.

> *Or let him take hold of My strength that he may make peace with Me: and he shall make peace with Me. Those who come He shall cause to take root in Jacob; Israel shall bloom and bud, and fill the face of the world with fruit.*

What kind of fruit do I believe will be flooding the face of the world? The good fruit of peace!

†

Speak and establish His peace in the realms around you.

As we look into other New Testament uses of *eirene* peace, we find Jesus sending out His disciples with instructions to literally speak peace before entering the homes in the towns they were sent to. This directive was given in Luke 10:1-10.

In verse 1, we're told Jesus appointed 70 disciples and sent them out two by two to the places where Jesus would soon be traveling. Clear instructions were given to them all as they prepared to depart. Carry no money bags, knapsacks, or extra sandals. Don't get caught up in long greetings as you travel, but stay focused on the purpose of your mission.

However in verses 5 and 6, Jesus says something very interesting. He says, *"But whatever house you enter, first say 'Peace to this house.' And if a son of peace is there, your peace will rest on it; if not, it will return to you."*

What is He referring to? I believe this is a direct reference to the peace Jesus gave us as a gift in John 14:27. This peace is completely different from cheap distractions, chemically-assisted states of numbness, and destructive passivity that we are often so familiar with. This gift of peace is one that enables us to join in unity with the peace of Heaven, which brings quietness, rest, and true prosperity.

This peace first comes upon us, and as we speak, it is released upon any home or individual who is open to the peace of God. Our gift of peace literally quiets the voices of the enemy so those under our "blanket of peace" can easily hear the Holy Spirit's voice as He addresses the issues He chooses in their lives (see Luke 10:6).

According to Luke 10:6, there will be occasions when this gift of peace simply will not come upon a person. I believe this has to do with the condition of that individual's heart. Hard-hearted people have already made up their minds not to yield to the voice of the Spirit. We see an example of that in First Samuel 25 where David sent his men to the house of Nabal to offer him greetings of peace in David's name.

David told his servants to greet Nabal by saying, *"Peace* [shalom] *be to you, peace to your house, and peace to all that you have"* (1 Sam. 25:6).

However, verse three describes Nabal as *"harsh and evil in his doings,"* while his wife, Abigail was *"a woman of good understanding and beautiful appearance."* His servants kindly made the request from this very wealthy man for some food to help David and his men during an upcoming Jewish feast day. He was reminded that the men of David helped to protect his flocks while they were shearing sheep in Carmel.

Nabal, true to the definition of his name and corresponding character traits, responded to David's offer of God's blessing and peace by acting as a fool. He said:

> *...Who is David, and who is the son of Jesse? There are many servants nowadays who break away each one from his master. Shall I then take my bread and my water and my meat that I have killed for my shearers, and give it to men when I do not know where they are from?* (1 Samuel 25:10-11)

First of all, let me assure you, Nabal knew very well who David was. David's fame as the giant-killer and war hero filled the land for many years prior. His marriage to King Saul's daughter and friendship with Jonathan, the king's son, was not to be overlooked. Nabal's harsh response was an intentional insult to David and his character.

Upon hearing this report, David was ready to retaliate.

There was one, however, who was wise in the midst of all this foolishness, and her name was Abigail. When Abigail heard of her husband's reviling of David's servants, she quickly jumped into action. She loaded up their donkeys with loaves of bread, wine, five sheep already prepared, roasted grain, clusters of raisins, and cakes of figs. Her servants were sent ahead to offer David and his men this feast on saddlebags while she rode behind.

When Abigail did meet David, she threw herself on the ground before him asking for forgiveness on behalf of Nabal, her husband. Her humility stopped David in his tracks. He suddenly realized that avenging himself was not God's way at all! He ended up thanking Abigail for both her courage and character to intervene.

In verse 35, David tells Abigail, *"Go up in peace* [shalom] *to your house. See I have heeded your voice and respected your person."*

The story continues with Abigail confronting her husband the next morning with all she had done in order to save their lives. We're told the heart of this harsh man literally died within him. Ten days later Nabal died (see 1 Sam. 25:1-38).

I share this story to help us visualize one who is not a "son of peace" or one who would not be open to the gift of shalom peace offered by David. Because David refrained from self-defense, the Lord was able to come in and bring His righteous judgment upon Nabal's life. In the New Testament, we find not just shalom peace offered, but now the gift of *eirene* peace, which has the ability to establish a person in unity with the Kingdom of peace.

†

Though eirene peace may be declared, not everyone always responds to this call.

Even with an increase of peace made available on the earth at this time, there still will be those who defiantly resist the call of the Spirit to make peace with the coming King. If they do not repent, they may suffer the same type of ending as Nabal. With each rejection, we're told the gift of peace will simply return to us.

In a modern scenario, I've literally seen those choosing paths of darkness experiencing great discomfort in the presence of peace. Sometimes the residing peace is so overwhelming that they feel as though they must flee. This type of response is not actually from the individual, but rather the darkness within them that has difficulty remaining in the light for very long (see Eph. 5:11-13).

We witnessed this once when a drug-using friend was convinced by his mother to come over to our house so we could speak with him. He was fine until he stepped onto our property. Once he came into our sphere of spiritual influence, the darkness in him panicked. He told us that it took everything within him just to keep from literally darting out our front door and running away. Fortunately, he resisted the temptation to flee and was able to receive some ministry that day.

Carrying the Gift of Peace to Others

Returning to our study of Luke 10, we see Jesus instructing the disciples to speak or declare this peace over every home they entered. When they found those who openly received their message of peace, they were instructed to stay and eat (or drink) whatever their hosts offered them. Jesus referred to this as part of the "wages" they were to receive while laboring in the Kingdom (see Luke 10:7).

The disciples were not to move from house to house, but to stay with their original hosts until they had completed their mission. Verse 8 repeats this same instruction, but makes reference to the entire town receiving their message of peace. In verse 9 they were told to *"heal the sick"* and say *"The kingdom of God has come near to you."* Again their emphasis was on speaking peace and then declaring that the Kingdom of God had brushed by their hearts. The listeners had the opportunity to respond.

The emphasis is also on speaking these things aloud. Matthew 10:5-13 repeats much of this same instruction, but tells the disciples to say *"The kingdom of heaven is at hand."* More detail is given for them to heal the sick, cleanse the lepers, raise the dead, and to cast out demons (see Matt. 10:8). Again, they are told not to bring extra money, bags, tunics, sandals, or even staffs. They were to completely step out in faith, trusting God for all their provision, and after greeting the people of that household, if they found it "worthy" or deserving, they were to bless it by extending their covering of peace upon it (see Matt. 10:13).

As we ponder the importance of speaking peace and declaring the Kingdom of Heaven, we can begin to see how much authority our words do carry with them. We can either speak death or idle or worthless words over people, or we can choose to speak life even while releasing the comforting peace of the Holy Spirit over a situation. By speaking in agreement with what is happening in Heaven, we can literally see or experience that release of God's power.

The choice is ours.

Jesus also spoke about the words coming out of our mouths in Matthew 12:34b-37. He said:

> *...For out of the abundance of the heart the mouth speaks. A good man out of the good treasure of his heart brings forth good things, and an evil man out of the evil treasure brings forth evil things. But I say to you that for every idle word men may speak, they will give account for it in the Day of Judgment. For by your words you will be justified, and by your words you will be condemned.*

Wow! Those verses alone are enough to make you stop and think!

You see, we each carry great authority whether we recognize it or not. Our words would be like those of a king who was just "fooling around" and accidently issued an execution order for an acquaintance of his! Does that sound like something we should take lightly?

No way!

We have been commissioned by the Eternal King to release Jesus' gift of peace into the lives of others around us. The Holy Spirit and all of the angelic messengers are waiting for us to speak life and truth so they can work to see these things established on the earth. This is our calling and our destiny.

I love the challenge of Moses to the children of Israel in regard to this. It says:

> *I call heaven and earth as witnesses today against you, that I have set before you life and death, blessing and cursing; therefore choose life that both you and your descendants may live...* (see Deuteronomy 30:19).

This call to life is still ringing and reverberating throughout the earth. We still have that choice as long as we reside on this planet. With everything within me, I encourage you to join me in choosing life, blessing, and the paths of peace laid out before us!

◆ ◆ ◆

Paths of Peace

I realize that for many of us, the idea of weighing every word that comes out of our mouths may appear a bit daunting, but in order for us to remain on the paths of peace the Lord has established, everything about us must be overcome with His peace, even our mouths! The Book of James talks about how necessary it is for us to "bridle" our tongues. If we do not conquer our minds and give evidence of this through our tongues, then James actually says our religion is useless (see James 1:26).

Ouch! That hurts so good!

It seems the whole point of a renewed mind is to speak and do things as led by the Spirit of God. We are called to release God's gift of peace over all who will accept it. How can we possibly do that if our tongues just randomly speak whatever pops into our minds, whether good or bad? That actually sounds a little scary to me! Our unbridled tongues could be dumping all kinds of word curses all over the people we love and are supposed to impact for Heaven!

I once heard a man of God say that every time we agree with a lie from hell, we are helping to build the kingdom of darkness and every time we fully embrace and walk in the truths of Heaven, we are part of establishing the Kingdom of Heaven on earth. That really hit me! I never want to assist the devil in any of his work! My only desire is to see the Kingdom of God released in me and around me wherever I go. I am confident that this is your desire as well.

Let's Pray

Dear Lord Jesus,

First, I want to thank you again for Your gift of peace. I don't ever want to take Your peace for granted, but want to fully embrace this gift while learning how to release Your peace into the lives of those around me. I am mindful of how You sent the disciples out with instructions to speak peace over every home they went to. Teach me how to speak this same peace over those You desire to impact with Your presence.

Forgive me, Lord, for every idle or worthless word I have spoken in the past. I ask You to forgive me for taking the authority You have given me lightly. Wash me clean in Your blood so this will not be held against me in the Day of Judgment. I receive Your forgiveness in my life over this area. Thank You!

Now I speak to the lie that says my words don't matter. I tell you in Jesus' name that I no longer believe this lie. Your power has been destroyed in me, and I send you and any other spirit that came in as a result of this lie to the feet of Jesus! Get out of me now!

Right now, I also break off every word curse that I have spoken over others in my ignorance. I declare that every careless word will fall to the ground and become as nothing. Instead of speaking death over my friends and family, I speak life and declare the goodness of God over each of their lives!

I invite the peace of the Lord Jesus Christ to now flood me and all those that I have previously cursed. Come Holy Spirit and fill every area of my life once more. Thank You so much for this peace that passes all understanding! Amen.

Chapter 10

COVERED IN PEACE

Once we had the privilege of meeting a man of God from Pennsylvania recognized as highly gifted in speaking words of peace wherever He went. Delivered from many years of drug addiction, Todd had been radically filled with the love of the Lord. His pure and sincere passion for God drove him to literally devour the Word of God, transforming his life.

His child-like obedience to the voice of the Lord led him to places where the prophetic fire of God bathed him in glory repeatedly. In the end, the love began pouring out of him, resulting in physical healings and life changes nearly every place he went.

Some healings occurred just by a hug!

As Todd was flying into our area to speak, my husband, John, was called upon to pick him up at the airport and then drive him out to the pastor's house where he would be staying. It was early morning when he arrived, so he and John decided to stop at a local restaurant for breakfast.

Soon after they were seated, the waitress came over to take their order. Todd suddenly asked if her back was hurting her. Surprised by his question, the waitress confirmed that it did hurt because her legs were not the same length and then asked if he was "clairvoyant."

Ignoring her response, Todd asked her to sit down so he could check. A bit confused, the woman sat down and extended her legs. Sure enough there was an inch and a half difference between the two. Todd prayed in the name of Jesus and commanded her short leg to grow. The waitress grew excited as she could feel her leg and muscles stretching as he prayed. Her legs were even!

Todd then asked her to stand up. While checking her back, he asked if she also had pain in her neck. Admitting that she did, he simply laid his hand upon her neck and asked Jesus to touch her neck as well.

The woman was speechless as she stood pain-free for the first time in years!

The two men ate their breakfast in great joy as they knew the Kingdom of Heaven was very near to this waitress. When it came time to pay for the meal (Todd insisted on paying for the breakfast!), once again he looked at the waitress and asked if she had suffered financially for the last couple of years.

She admitted she had.

The Lord had informed him of her financial difficulties, and at that point Todd decided to "sow" into her finances. He added a one hundred dollar tip to the tab.

Shocked, the waitress didn't know what to do! At first, she had a hard time accepting that large of a tip, but eventually she did. Not knowing what to do, she reached over and gave Todd a hug and then had to walk away as she fought tears. Todd declared that the waitress would never be the same again. He knew that the Holy Spirit would not let her go.

The waitress had encountered the healing love of Jesus.

†

The healing love of Jesus sown in peace brought forth fruit in her life.

From there, the two men stopped by our house briefly in order to pick me up so I could join them on their journey to Port Orchard where he was staying. Soon after I met Todd, he asked if I was suffering from a neck injury.

Though I had not experienced pain from my neck in quite a while (I had been healed from neck pain many years before), I could still hear crackling and crunching of bones every time I moved my head. Previous X-rays had shown I had several whiplash-damaged vertebrae from a couple of car accidents I had experienced years ago.

Todd prayed a simple prayer. We left soon after that. It was several hours later before I realized that I could move my head around without any sounds of grinding bones at all. That was amazing!

The love and peace Todd walked in caused him to move very naturally into his everyday surroundings and bring with him the healing presence of the Lord. Prayers for healing shouldn't just happen in churches or behind closed doors. The Lord wants us to boldly carry His gifts everywhere we go.

Todd didn't have to preach a sermon to the waitress that day. She saw for herself the love of God made manifest in her presence. Todd's contagious joy and peace captured her heart. He knew it was the Holy Spirit's job to finish what had already begun in that young woman's heart.

We can see this same pattern of peace-filled love impacting people while walking the streets of Israel in the Acts of the Apostles. People were healed even as Peter's shadow touched the sick (see Acts 5:15). Many people in this day and age have "heard" about Jesus and the Bible, but few have actually encountered the life-changing power of the Father's love revealed in their lives. I believe it is time for all of us to learn how to be conduits of the Lord's love and power flowing through clear channels of peace established within us!

Thomas à Kempis (1380-1471), a medieval Catholic monk, also believed that inner peace with God had to come first before we should attempt to bring peace to others. Thought to be the probable author of *The Imitation of Christ,* one of the best-known Christian books on devotion, Thomas was quoted as saying, "First keep the peace within yourself then you can also bring peace to others."[1]

Credited as a prolific copyist and writer, Thomas is believed to have hand-copied the entire Bible at least four times during his quiet years of prayer, reflection, and writing. Another pearl of wisdom often attributed to Thomas is, "Without the Way, there is no going; Without the Truth, there is no knowing; Without the Life, there is no living."[2]

While noting his wisdom based on our knowledge of Jesus as the Way, the Truth, and the Life, I might also add that evidence of this life within us should also be displayed with an abundance of peace (see John 14:6). I still can remember that first night several years ago when the Holy Spirit began instructing me about peace.

Discovering the Treasury of Peace We've Been Given

Having trouble getting to sleep one night, I quietly got out of our bed so as not to disturb my sleeping husband and came downstairs. The topic of peace had been swirling around in my head for some time so I decided to begin looking up the verses discussing peace.

What I discovered astounded me!

I found several pages of my *Strong's Concordance* filled with references to peace! Previously, I had not been aware of that many peace references in the Bible. As I was determined to study all God had to say on this topic, I began reading and writing down each of the references into the various categories they fell into. (That is how this book came into existence!)

Hour after hour, I continued to read and write, absolutely fascinated with what I was learning. The Holy Spirit was speaking so fast at times it was difficult to write as quickly as He was communicating. It was truly an amazing night.

While working my way through the Old Testament, the Gospels, the book of Acts, and into the Epistles, I began noticing a curious pattern. In most of the letters somewhere in the beginning and ending portions of each Epistle, words of peace (and often grace) were spoken over the readers.

For example, Romans 1:7 says: *"To all who are in Rome, beloved of God, called to be saints: Grace to you and* ***peace*** *from God our Father and the Lord Jesus Christ."*

Now let's look at Romans 16:19-20.

> *For your obedience has become known to all. Therefore I am glad on your behalf; but I want you to be wise in what is good and simple concerning evil. And the God of* ***peace*** *will crush Satan under your feet shortly. The* ***grace*** *of our Lord Jesus be with you. Amen.*

It's interesting to note Paul's indication that it is the God of peace who enables us to crush satan under our feet. Also, the word used for *grace* is *charis* in the Greek, which is defined as "graciousness, and the divine influence on the heart."[3]

However, this word also means "cheerful or calmly happy or well-off." That sure sounds like godly peace to me!

Let me list several more for you.

> *Grace to you and peace from God our Father and the Lord Jesus Christ* (1 Corinthians 1:3).
>
> *The grace of our Lord Jesus Christ be with you* (1 Corinthians 16:23).
>
> *Grace to you and peace from God our Father and the Lord Jesus Christ* (2 Corinthians 1:2).
>
> *Finally, my brethren, farewell. Become complete. Be of good comfort, be of one mind, live in peace; and the God of love and peace will be with you* (2 Corinthians 13:11).
>
> *Grace to you and peace from God the Father and our Lord Jesus Christ* (Galatians 1:3).
>
> *For in Christ Jesus neither circumcision nor uncircumcision avails anything, but a new creation. And as many as walk according to this rule, peace and mercy be upon them, and upon the Israel of God* (Galatians 6:15-16).

The list continues on with nearly each epistle declaring its proclamation of peace or grace over those reading the words of Paul and the other writers. The only exceptions I've found are in the books of James and Jude. In the writings of John, we find another variation of the word for *grace* translated as *joy* in First John 1:4.[4] Though we don't necessarily see John ending his letters with peace or joy, each of his three letters does make reference to this *chara* joy in the beginning.

As I pondered all of this, the Holy Spirit seemed to indicate that peace, grace, and joy were first written at the beginning so the truths of the letters could be easily communicated to the reader. Words of peace, grace, and joy were then at the end to help seal the written truths within their hearts, helping to prevent the enemy from coming in to steal what had been taught.

Spoken or written words of peace do not only impact our lives physically. The world around us is also impacted by peace. In both Luke 8:23 and Mark 4:39, we see Jesus first rebuking the winds and then speaking peace to the seas. The moment the words of peace came out of His mouth, the sea responded by immediately becoming calm.

We're told in Romans 8:19-21 that all of creation is groaning for and eagerly awaiting the full revelation of the sons of God. Verse 19 says, *"For the earnest expectation of the creation eagerly waits for the revealing of the sons of God."* Verse 21 states, *"because the creation itself also will be delivered from the bondage of corruption into the glorious liberty of the children of God."*

Could Jesus be referring to this kind of peaceful authority in Matthew 17:20? He said:

> *...If you have faith as a mustard seed, you will say to this mountain, "Move from here to there," and it will move; and nothing will be impossible for you.*

These verses indicate that we can and will have an impact upon nature around us. Creation yearns for us to use our words of peace to help reconcile all of nature back to its beloved Creator! A trespasser, a usurper, has come in to try and destroy all peace from this earth, but the Father has raised us up as His rightful heirs so that the Kingdom of peace can be reestablished on the earth—first in our own hearts, then in the hearts of those around us, and then within creation itself.

It is our right. It is our duty!

Isaiah 55:12 lays out before us a picture of what our lives can and should look like as all of creation responds to the sons and daughters of God. It says:

> *For you shall go out with joy, and be led out with peace; the mountains and the hills shall break forth into singing before you, and all the trees of the field shall clap their hands.*

Imagine what our world might be like with a whole entourage of sons and daughters of God bringing and establishing peace wherever they go! Storms would stop before us. The mountains and hills would respond to our commands. Walking on water or going through walls would seem as nothing. Calling forth rains in the right season and declaring droughts would be a part of our responsibility here on earth. Animals would no longer fear us as they would sense the presence of their Creator upon us.

†

Even creation is waiting for us to use God's authority in establishing peace.

And all of this would only be preparation for the wonderful responsibilities awaiting us in eternity!

Listen to the words of King David as he captures in poetic verse the interaction of God as He seeks to establish His wonderful flow of peace within the life of a believer. Psalm 85:8-13 says:

> *I will hear what God will speak, for He will speak peace to His people and to His saints; but let them not turn back to folly. Surely His salvation is near to those who fear Him that glory may dwell in our land. Mercy and truth have met together. Righteousness and peace have kissed. Truth shall spring out of the earth, and righteousness shall look down from heaven. Yes, the Lord will give what is good; and our land will yield its increase. Righteousness will go before Him, and shall make His footsteps our pathway.*

By examining this poem, we see an indication that God is speaking peace to His people. If we leave the paths of peace, we will find ourselves back to folly. The glorious presence of the Lord is released upon the land through those who have received His gift of salvation through Jesus.

When we submit to the sword of peace, as described in an earlier chapter, lies are exposed and truth is presented to us. Once we admit our sin, the Lord is able to offer His mercy to us through the blood of Jesus. Our sin is removed by His sacrifice and truth replaces the lies.

Once righteousness has been established in our lives, we are "kissed" by peace. We are at peace with the Kingdom of peace. As we speak and establish truth in our realms of influence, Heaven will respond by causing even the land to become fruitful in our lives.

Notice the last line of this passage. We are told that when the Father looks upon us, He will only see the righteousness of His Son upon us, and we will literally be *"making His footsteps our pathway."* By agreeing and holding on to peace, we will find ourselves walking the pathways of Jesus on this earth!

Isn't that exciting?

This is a beautiful picture of how the Father longs to interact with each of us! "Let My peace flow in you and through you," He says. "I want each of you to experience the love, intimacy, and joy that come when you are walking in My pathways of peace."

How could we possibly refuse such an amazing offer?

♦ ♦ ♦

Paths of Peace

Sometimes when we are presented with a prophetic picture that is beyond our current understanding, the tendency is to discount the truths presented as unachievable. The establishment of peace in our lives, however, is not unachievable, but entirely possible. The work begins by disciplining our minds to fully embrace truth rather than the lies we often pick up while trudging through the evil and darkness still working on this earth. Once the lies have been identified, it takes a conscious effort to dislodge the lies by flooding ourselves with His truth.

When the truth has convinced us of who we really are, we can begin by speaking peace over our own lives. If we find ourselves lacking in one area, we only need to first ask the Lord to apply His sword to our hearts so we can see what lie we have agreed with. Exercising the wonderful gift of repentance, we will be cleansed and set at one again with the Lord. The Book of James encourages us to ask freely for whatever we need, promising that the Lord will lavish His answer upon us (see James 1:5).

How can we fail?

Our goal is to learn the paths of peace so we can bring the wonderful news of peace to this world around us. We are the heirs of the God of Peace, the Prince of Peace, and the Spirit of

Peace. It is fully within our capabilities to learn how to speak, write, and establish peace wherever we go.

All of creation has its eyes upon us, desiring for us to work in agreement with the Father. His paths of peace are before us. His kiss of peace awaits us. We only need to begin exercising the peace He has given us so that His peace will increase with use (see Heb. 5:14).

Let's Pray

Dear Lord Jesus,

By examining all the uses and promises given to me by walking in peace, I understand the high level of importance You have placed upon this gift. I desire Your peace in every area of my life. I want to understand how to begin speaking peace in every realm of my influence, whether it be at home or out in public. Your word says that even creation responds to peace. Teach me how to exercise this gift!

As Your ambassador on this earth, I understand it is my duty to guard every word that comes out of my mouth. Only You can help me carry this God-given authority with love and compassion, but most especially as led by the Holy Spirit.

Holy Spirit, I invite You to take control of my

mouth. I desire to only speak words of life and not death. I don't want to have empty or profitless words pollute even the air around me. I declare that You are able to lead me in paths of peace and instruct me in how to establish God's peace around me.

Thank You so much for leading and guiding me in every area of my life. Amen.

Chapter 11

MOUNTAINS OF PEACE

One evening, I was invited to speak at a local church for their Wednesday night bible study group. When the invitation was first extended, the pastor forewarned me that Wednesday night typically consisted of a smaller group that often wanted to finish up rather early so they could hurry home. I was fine with that and decided beforehand just to allow the Holy Spirit to have His way regardless of the numbers.

As I prayed about what message I should focus on for that evening, the Holy Spirit seemed to indicate that I should teach about the peace of God. During my preparation process, I realized that I would never be able to fully cover everything involved with this topic, so I put together a very general introduction encouraging those meeting with us to really research the peace of God more thoroughly on their own.

That night at the church, both the pastor and I were amazed at the number of people packed into this smaller room. Many local people had heard about my first book, *The 12 Gemstones of Revelation,* and were anxious to hear me speak.

Once I started the ministry of the Word, there seemed to be no problem in holding the interest of that group. In fact, in an effort to honor the pastor's wishes to close the meeting at a reasonable hour, I ended the teaching portion of the ministry so those needing to could leave before the prayer time.

No one left.

Prior to the beginning of the service, the Holy Spirit had given me specific instructions as to what to pray for that evening, primarily focusing on those struggling with overwhelming fears. When I began calling out the prayer focuses I had been given, I was amazed at the number of people who responded.

Nearly every person in the room came forward for prayer, most of them admitting a huge struggle in the area of fear!

†

The number of Christians lacking peace and battling overwhelming fears surprised me!

It was much later that night before I could even see an end to individuals wanting prayer. Amazingly, as always, the Holy

Spirit touched many lives that evening, bringing healing and freedom to those willing to admit their need.

When I was finally able to leave for home that night, I was greatly impacted by the numbers of Christians struggling with fears in many areas of their lives. Since that time, I have even had others who, upon hearing about the topic of this book, asked me how soon this material might be available. It is obvious that the manifestation of supernatural peace in the lives of believers is something many are crying out for in this stress-filled world.

On another occasion, I had the opportunity to speak with a lovely young Korean woman who had flown out to our church in order to receive some needed prayer. As we spoke, I began sharing some of the recent lessons I had gleaned in my studies on peace. She listened wide-eyed as I described the response I had seen among local Christians as I shared about the importance of God's peace within our lives.

Knowing that she had traveled other nations, I asked if the lack of peace within the lives of Christians was a problem she had noticed as well.

"Oh yes," she assured me.

The woman indicated it was a problem in Korea and the other countries she had visited as well. I could see that God's peace was something she was seeking in regards to her plans for the future. She needed to be led by His peace in her decisions. This is why she had come.

Jesus Exhorted Each of Us Not to Worry

We can be thankful that the Lord, aware of our need for peace, has already given us everything we need to attain it. Jesus has given us very clear instructions on how to position our minds to be recipients of His peace. His discourse on worry found in Luke 12:22-34 offers several keys necessary in releasing the old fears and replacing them with the truths about the Kingdom of peace.

- We are more important than creation.

When speaking to His disciples, Jesus began by telling them, "*...Do not worry about your life, what you will eat; nor about the body, what you will put on*" (Luke 12:22). Life is so much more than food and clothing, He tells us. Just look at the birds of the air. Not one of them has a storehouse of grain stored up for a "rainy day," and yet they are always fed. If the birds are taken care of, how much more will He care for our needs?

- Are we striving to accomplish things in our own power or relying upon God?

Consider the flowers of the fields. They grow and are gloriously arrayed without a bit of striving. If our God is fully capable of caring for every living thing on this earth, how much more will He care for those of us created in His image!

Honestly, the major difference between nature and us is the fact that we can consider and entertain many thoughts. The thoughts we meditate on and embrace dictate whether we will trust the Creator or attempt to take care of things ourselves.

- Has the anchor of faith been lifted in our minds?

In verse 29, Jesus warns about having an anxious or doubtful mind. The word used for this is *meteorizo* and indicates a fluctuating mind, one which has lifted the anchor of faith and is now drifting as the lies continue to blow us off course.[1]

In verse 32, Jesus again tells us, *"Do not fear, little flock, for it is the Father's good pleasure to give you the kingdom."*

We can see that fear, worry, and anxiousness are the very things that rob us of our hope and confidence in what the Father has said is true! The enemy is the one throwing lies, cares, and doubts at us. If we choose to believe the enemy, we are allowing him to have his way in our lives, and his paths lead to loss, death, and utter destruction. Obviously, paths of peace are much preferred to the alternative!

Not only are we called to remain on God's paths of peace, we are similarly called to become as "mountains of peace" in a world fraught with fear. The Lord's "peace process" is laid out for us in Isaiah 40, where the prophet describes the things God will do in the lives of His saints.

The prophet Isaiah tells us that in order to be prepared as God's "highway of holiness," every valley in our lives must be lifted up (see Isa. 40:3-4). These valleys represent every thought of insignificance or inferiority that we have agreed with. God actually sees this as a form of arrogance.[2]

As those lies are broken off, the Holy Spirit then goes after our "mountains of pride." The mountains here refer to every high and lofty thought we have agreed with about ourselves in some way. Often this is apparent when we think of our abilities as self-made or superior to others. Sometimes pride can show up when we think we have to do things or promote ourselves rather than relying upon God.[3]

Once pride has been demolished, the Holy Spirit will begin examining any "crooked" ways we have incorporated into our thinking. Crooked ways might include religious or unnecessary requirements we have put on ourselves or others in order to make ourselves appear more holy before God or others. Crooked ways are also described as "torturous"[4] when contrasted with the ways of peace God has actually called us to.

Next, the Holy Spirit begins His work on our "rough places." Rough places are described as mountain ridges where the summits are all tied together.[5] These "points of resistance" might be better portrayed as ungodly soul ties. Anytime we have closely tied connections with those who are resistant to God's ways, we will find ourselves drawn to follow our friends rather than follow God. The need for separation is apparent when one desires to learn a new way of living in agreement with the Holy Spirit.

While still in high school, I can remember meeting a young woman who appeared to be spiritually dark and very needy. I immediately assumed that it was my job to minister to her. This "friendship" continued for many months as I continued to meet with her in hopes to see her life turned around.

Instead of seeing victory and changes in her life, I noticed a change in my own behavior. Every time I met with her, I felt exhausted and drained.

Depression began to set in.

As I prayed about the situation, I realized that this was an unhealthy relationship where the darkness my friend had chosen as an attention-getting method was impacting me. If I did not meet with her when she called, I often was troubled by feelings of guilt.

Finally, the Holy Spirit allowed me to understand that the control or ungodly soul tie with this girl had to be severed. I was to turn this burden over to the Lord so He could deal with her as He chose. Once that decision was made, I began feeling much better and was able to continue on my own path toward spiritual maturity.

Any ungodly soul ties where we find ourselves responding more in guilt and yielding to the control of others need to be made into an open and wide plain of separation. Though we can still see these resistant souls around us, we are not to closely associate with them, but rather focus on developing our new love and passion for the Lord.

Once these steps have been taken, we will be able to see the glory of the Lord revealed in our lives (see Isa. 40:5). The clearing and destruction of all resistance to the Lord will permit the peace of God to begin permeating every part of our lives. We have made peace with the God of peace, and His highway is now flowing through us!

The next instructions we are given can be found in Isaiah 40:9, where the Spirit of God calls out to all who are now able to adequately bring good tidings to others. He says:

> *O Zion, you who bring good tidings, get up into the high mountain; O Jerusalem, you who bring good tidings, lift up your voice with strength, lift it up, be not afraid; say to the cities of Judah, "Behold your God!"*

When we compare this verse to Jesus' discourse in Matthew 5:14-16, there are some striking similarities. Jesus told us:

> *You are the light of the world. A city that is set on a hill cannot be hidden. Nor do they light a lamp and put it under a basket, but on a lampstand, and it gives light to all who are in the house. Let your light so shine before men, that they may see your good works and glorify your Father in heaven.*

I believe these verses describe one who has made peace with God and has now become a peacemaker in the Kingdom of God. Our gift of peace literally looms up as a huge mountain in the face of those still in bondage to fear. This mountainous peace we carry calls to them, and they are drawn to ask us the reason for our peace.

Listen again to the words found in Isaiah 52:7 as the prophet describes the beauty of those living as this mountain of peace.

> *How beautiful upon the mountains are the feet of him who brings good news, who proclaims peace, who brings glad tidings of good things, who proclaims salvation, who says to Zion, "Your God reigns."*

King Solomon also describes those who have established themselves as "mountains of peace" within this world. Psalm 72:3 says, *"The mountains will bring peace to the people, and the little hills, by righteousness."*

In other words, Solomon is saying that those filled with the peace of God through the gift of His righteousness will assist in helping others to make peace with God as well, even encouraging those whose peace has only been to the level of "little hills." Several verses later, Solomon declares that *"in His days"* the righteous saints will flourish with an abundance of peace until the moon no longer exists (see Ps. 72:7).

Wow! That sounds encouraging!

Isaiah 54:10 gives further insight into the longevity of this wonderful covenant of peace we have established with our Creator. It says:

> *"For the mountains shall depart, and the hills removed, but My kindness shall not depart from you, nor shall My covenant of peace be removed," says the Lord, who has mercy on you.*

Making a Difference in the World Around Us

After reading through all these promises of peace, one might wonder if our mountain of peace might actually make a difference in the real world around us. I have wondered about this myself in the past, so the Lord granted me the opportunity to see how His peace functions in very carnal or natural settings.

†

We become as obvious as a mountain when we walk in God's covenant of peace.

Following 13 years of homeschooling our four children, then teaching and working in a Christian school, I found myself seeking part-time employment at a location near our home. I walked into the offices of Skip Barber Racing School and spoke to the office manager. Yes, she told me, she could use some assistance as a receptionist and store manager. Soon I found myself working in an environment that I found to be completely alien to the one I had lived in for so many years!

For those unfamiliar with the professional racing crowd, often the lifestyle and "rough" language coming out of the mouths of the staff, employees, and clients are quite a contrast to what many Christians are accustomed to. At first, I experienced quite a "culture shock" as I observed the "wild ways" of those I was working among, especially after coming directly from working at a church and Christian school!

The Lord, however, was merciful to me, and soon I learned how to maintain the peace of God even in that very difficult environment. When working as the receptionist, I had my computer quietly playing online Christian music in the background. My prayers for those around me became very focused as I endeavored simply to love them as Jesus loved them.

I first began to notice a difference in the mechanics whenever they happened to step into the office at various times throughout the day. Often they would walk in and begin speaking to one of the other employees in their normal foul language, but once they noticed that I was behind the desk, they immediately apologized and attempted to speak in a "cleaner" fashion.

I had never said one word about their language or their lifestyles at that point. I only prayed. The realization that someone else was working upon their hearts gave me great encouragement.

Another time, the office manager, Janette,[6] called me into her office to give me some instructions for the day. Halfway through our discussion, she stopped and commented that she noticed every time I was working behind the desk, the whole building felt much more peaceful. I briefly explained to her that I was a Christian and the peace came from Jesus. At that, she politely smiled and quickly changed the topic of our discussion.

Though Janette was not open to the good news at that time, there was one who was.

One morning, I was working in a side room directly off the front office. There I was separating, tagging, and folding shirts to be sold in our small merchandise store on the premises. At a table across the room sat one of the professional drivers staring at the laptop in front of him working on some kind of project.

Not wanting to disturb him, I silently folded the merchandise, but began praying under my breath for this young man. After awhile, I couldn't help but notice his somewhat downcast expression. Gathering my courage, I decided to ask what was bothering him.

Amazingly, Steve[7] opened up and began sharing some of his deep, heart-felt frustrations in living the lifestyle expected from a professional race car driver. It turned out that Steve had been a Christian, but after several years of being in the limelight, he had succumbed to the many temptations of sin he was surrounded by. The guilt of his failures had overshadowed the fame and fortune that often follows those in his shoes.

We spoke for quite some time before I realized that I needed to leave shortly for home, so I encouraged Steve to drive up to our motor home where we had been staying so he could pray with both my husband and me about his spiritual condition. I left the office that day in intense prayer on his behalf. Steve needed to step out and act upon the things I had shared with him, proving that he was serious about his desire for change.

Later that afternoon, Steve drove up and parked in front of our old motor home. I have to admit, it was a bit humbling to have this well-known driver come into our 33-foot "home" in order to pray with us. As sincerely as he could, Steve prayed with us, confessing his sin and asking Jesus to forgive him and wash him clean in His blood.

When he finished, there was a definite change in his countenance. The guilt and shame were gone. There was a definite sense of relief he experienced as the darkness lifted off of him.

After discussing some options for him to remain accountable, Steve assured us that he would get back in contact with his home church so they could encourage him in his faith even while he maintained his busy travel schedule. He left that day with a much larger smile on his face.

John and I were honored that day to be used by God as mountains of peace in the life of one who had been sidetracked and deceived by the enemy. It was the peace of God that drew Steve to me and his hunger for peace in his own life that brought him to our motor home that afternoon. His prayers of surrender brought him to terms with the Prince of Peace, allowing the comforter to bring the needed resolution in his heart.

A new peace was established in Steve's life, one that I am certain he will guard with all diligence.

After experiencing the establishment of my mountain of peace in such a dark environment, I have grown more and more confident in the effectiveness of heavenly peace as the "draw card" for a world starved for true peace only found in Jesus' gift to us as believers. It is the working of both *eirene* and *shalom* peace in our lives that causes all the gifts of the Spirit to literally shine before the world.

When we walk in peace, the whole world will stop and take note.

John Wooden, a retired American basketball coach, has the distinction of being a member of the Basketball Hall of Fame as both a player (class of 1961) and as a coach (class of 1973). John is also a man of great faith who has authored a number of books on success.[8] Commenting on the illusive mental peace so many are in pursuit of, he said, "There are many things essential to arriving at true peace of mind, and one of the most important is faith, which cannot be acquired without prayer."[9]

The world has taken notice of this great man of faith as he lived a life that first and foremost focused on his love and faith in God. John once said that he hopes his faith is apparent to others, declaring, "If I were ever prosecuted for my religion, I truly hope there would be enough evidence to convict me."[10]

The faith and peace John Wooden made reference to is available to all of us if we are willing to diligently pursue it. The Lord desires us to permanently reside in His peaceful habitations (see Isa. 32:17). In fact, the Lord actually wants to "delight us" with an abundance of His peace (see Ps. 37:8-9,11). This abundantly peaceful habitation is found only by permitting the Kingdom of peace to reside within us.

The Peace Pact We Must Enter Into

Dwight L. Moody (1837-1899) was an American evangelist and publisher who founded the Moody Church, the Northfield Mount Herman School in the state of Massachusetts, the Moody Bible Institute, and Moody Publishers. This great man of God once offered his insight on peace, saying, "A great many people are trying to make peace, but that has already been done. God has not left it for us to do; all we have to do is enter into it."[11]

Moody truly states that we in and of ourselves cannot create the peace we all desire; however, the mental work required to guard God's gift of peace is something we must diligently maintain. Hebrews 4 describes this place of spiritual rest or peace for us.

Maintaining peace with God in this chaotic world is not something that comes easily at first, but as we learn the skills required to fight and resist every lie attempting to rob us of the truth, it will become easier. Daily battles are won by remembering to test and examine every thought that comes to mind, determining whether or not it is in agreement with the Kingdom of God.

Of course, we would never be able to accurately discern truth or error without the Word of God or the Spirit of God quickening the truth within our hearts. This is something we all can and must ask the Lord, even as we study the Word of God for ourselves. This type of request thrills our Heavenly Father to answer in our lives!

†

The increasing peace within us indicates the lies have been uprooted.

In the beginning of God's peace process, we will soon find the Holy Spirit applying the sword of peace to our lives, exposing any and all lies that we have agreed with throughout the years. Often these lies have roots way back in our childhood where someone in ignorance told us that we were less than God intended.

As the lies are exposed, we can quickly repent of, rebuke, and destroy any strongholds created by these lies. When the lie has been revealed, our repentance grants us the authority to cast those lies out and replace them with the truth. Once this has been accomplished, we simply invite the Holy Spirit to flood this newly vacated area with His peace.

In learning a "safe and delivered" method of thinking, we must develop attentiveness and an intense watching for the return of familiar lies that we previously battled. The lies need to be "captured" and cast down as quickly as they attempt to reclaim territory in our minds. At times we may run across a "stronghold" or reinforced patterns of negative thinking that must be destroyed. This is accomplished by asking the Holy Spirit for assistance.

To begin walking out in peace, we are all encouraged to first shod our feet with peace. "Shod" has to do with wrapping our minds with the ways of peace or learning to only walk when peace is leading us. This indicates a time of preparation to attain this mindset. If we are not experiencing the peace of God, it is time to ask the Holy Spirit to show us what is out of order. By wrapping ourselves with this mindset of peace, we will be able to maintain God's peace regardless of what is going on around us.

As we learn to hear the Holy Spirit's direction in all we do, we can actually discover a sense of warning when we are beginning to depart from paths of peace. This is accomplished by the Sentinel of Peace. His forewarnings are invaluable! Much pain and sorrow can be averted when we heed the voice of Wisdom. The peace of the Holy Spirit desires to lead us and even act as the ruler or umpire in determining whether or not we should go in a certain direction (see Col. 3:15).

Once we've prepared ourselves against the attacks of fear, we can then begin taking ground in the Spirit each time we face down a lie that tries to assault us and instead establish a stronghold of peace in that area. When ground has been taken, it's actually a bit easier to defend your position of truth. You will not waver once you are fully convinced in your heart of God's truth in a particular area.

When learning about peace, we did establish the huge difference between living in peace and living in passivity. The two are simply miles apart from each other! Passivity is doing nothing, while the ways of peace require a very active and sharp mind that is constantly testing every thought that enters. Once an intruder has been discovered, the lie must be dealt with severely and replaced with the truth.

†

Living as a "peacemaker" is crucial for us and others while on earth.

When learning to walk in the paths of peace, there will come a time when we are ministering to others that we carry with us the authority to establish peace in their lives as well. We saw Jesus do this after several of the women He ministered to were sent off in peace. This spoken word of peace actually causes the person we might be praying for to be "set at one again" with the Kingdom of peace. Peace will not settle where a lie is still lodged; often spoken peace will cause the lie to surface so it can be properly dealt with before peace actually can settle on a person.

This truly is the beginning of us becoming peacemakers of God!

An often overlooked instruction given by Jesus to the disciples is when He directed them to literally speak peace over every home that they entered so that if the residents were open to the good news, the lies of the enemy would be silenced for a time so the truth could be spoken. If a person rejected the peace carried by the disciple, they were simply instructed to receive back their gift of peace, shake the dust (or spirit of rejection) off their own feet, and move on to the next place.

In the same way, we must learn to speak peace everywhere we go and watch for those who will respond to the call of the Holy Spirit so we can minister truth to them. Rejections will occur, but we cannot allow any type of offense in our lives, which will rob us of our peace.

The covering residual of peace is not only to be spoken over people and places around us. It can also be written as we learned by examining most of the epistles in the New Testament. Most of the epistles begin and end with declarations of peace, grace, or joy, which all make reference to a type of deep-rooted calming joy that comes from knowing and fully embracing the truth about God and ourselves. This gift of spiritual "charisma" is something one can live and walk in only when we are in full agreement with the Kingdom of peace.

As we learn to remain fully engaged with the Prince of Peace and His truths, the Word of God promises that we will become as mountains of peace in the eyes of the world. They will not be able to ignore the bright light emanating from within as we set captives free everywhere we go. Nor do we want them to!

It is part of spiritual inheritance to walk and live in this incredible, world-changing peace. The more of us who take the challenge to pursue these paths of peace, the more the world will see without a shadow of a doubt that we truly are the heirs of our Heavenly Father.

The world is waiting. All of creation is waiting. Heaven itself is waiting. Will you join me in this pursuit of our Kingdom of peace?

◆ ◆ ◆

Paths of Peace

In learning the ways of truly becoming a peacemaker in the Kingdom of God, we must first become well-acquainted with the paths of peace in our own lives. Matthew 5:9 tells us, *"Blessed are the peacemakers, for they shall be called sons of God."*

As the sons and daughters of God, if we have learned His ways, we will be both walking in personal peace and establishing peace in the lives of others around us. This is what we all want.

Jesus knew that maintaining a heart of faith would be a battle on earth, especially as the end grows closer. He spoke of this in Luke 18:8 where He asked if, when He returned, He would really find faith on the earth. I don't see this verse as discouraging, but rather as an encouragement for each of us to personally make the acquisition of this confident faith a priority and something we have grasped in our own lives.

The word used for faith here is *pistis*, and it refers to that same kind of persuasion and conviction I have been referring to throughout this book as the necessary mindset to ward off fear.[12] We must each learn to become absolutely convinced and fully reliant with complete certainty upon the promises of our Heavenly Father without one ounce of doubt or worry permitted within our minds.

That is the will of our Father; it is one of the spoken promises of Jesus; and it is fully within the capabilities of the Holy Spirit to accomplish it within our lives! All we need to do is ask for His peace. We must seek His peace in every area and know confidently that, if we knock, the Lord promises to open the door to us. He will never leave us or forsake us (see Heb. 13:5).

Let's Pray

Dear Lord Jesus,

I come before You in absolute surrender, especially in the area of my mind. I realize that the establishment of peace in my life is crucial to my becoming both a peacemaker and a son or daughter walking the paths of peace while on this earth. You have made it apparent that this is Your will for me and that You have given me all I need to accomplish Your purposes on this earth.

I want to become as a mountain of peace before the world so that Your light can brightly shine before all men. You have declared that this new form of Sabbath rest is what You have called all of us into, and it is my desire to enter into Your rest.

You have promised that if I ask, You will answer, so I humbly ask that You do all you need to do in me to transform my mind into one that is fully in agreement with the Kingdom of Heaven. Show me any lies that I am yet in agreement with so I can quickly repent, destroy them, and cast them out.

Holy Spirit, I give You full permission to turn on the searchlight of truth and examine every issue of my life. I want to hold nothing back from You. Reveal and help me remove any hindrance that is yet holding me back from the pristis faith I need to overcome this world. I choose to repent from those lies right now. Forgive me, Lord.

Enemy, I remind you that you are defeated and no longer have any hold upon me in the area of fear. I declare all your lies null and void in my life. I destroy every stronghold from the past and command that every spirit behind those lies must leave me now! I no longer want you in my life! Go!

Thank you, Heavenly Father, for Your continuing love and mercy following me every step of the way. I receive all of Your goodness and grace made available to me from the moment of my salvation. I declare that You are good and full of loving kindness.

I now declare that I am a person of peace. I will walk in full assurance of the truths spoken to me by the Spirit of God. I will overcome every lie and temptation attempting to draw me back into my old fears. I am a mountain of peace and a peacemaker on this earth. I know I am fully victorious in Christ Jesus! Amen!

Chapter 12

PEACEFUL WATERS

As we conclude our study on the weapons of peace God has given us, I thought it might be appropriate to take another look at Psalm 23 in lieu of our new understanding regarding peace. Once we apply the glasses of peace to our approach to this classic Sunday school memory piece, the whole psalm seems to open up before us.

Let's examine this verse by verse. Verse 1 says, *"The Lord is my shepherd; I shall not want."*

When considering the Lord's role as our shepherd, we see that He becomes much more than a distant ruler. He becomes a friend and close associate, one who literally walks with us through every challenge and hardship we may face.[1] We are never alone, and His provision for us will never lessen at any time in our lives.[2]

Verse 2 says, *"He makes me to lie down in green pastures; He leads me beside the still waters."*

The Lord literally will adjust our thinking in order to bring forth all we need in order to learn how to fully rest and recline in Him.[3] His purpose is to lead us into the beauty and pleasant habitation that He originally designed us for.[4] As we learn His ways of peace, we will discover the peace-filled living waters beginning to spring up from in the midst of us.[5]

Verse 3 says, *"He restores my soul; He leads me in the paths of righteousness for His name's sake."*

Simply because of His own mercy toward us and His understanding of the weakness within our flesh, the Holy Spirit works to lead us back into the paths of peace every time we stray. Each time He does this, our spiritual vitality and hunger for God returns.

By jubilantly running with us in the Spirit, Jesus causes us to literally sparkle and light up with His glory every time we return to His designated paths of peace.[6] These paths are not hidden, but rather placed in an elevated location, allowing others to find them who may be looking.[7] The way of peace actually acts as a fortification around us, causing us to prosper within the Kingdom of peace as our hearts and minds grow clearer in the Spirit.[8]

Verse 4 says, *"Yea, though I walk through the valley of the shadow of death, I will fear no evil; for You are with me; Your rod and Your staff, they comfort me."*

Yes, even though we may walk through some very dark-looking circumstances, we have nothing to fear. The peace of God has so permeated our minds that we have learned not to base our thoughts and decisions upon how things appear in the natural, but upon which direction the peace of God is leading us.

†

Spiritual vitality from walking on paths of peace causes us to sparkle with life.

The rod God uses to correct us every step of the way reminds us of the family of peace and authority we have now become a part of.[9] That understanding gives us great support and a sense of protection even when there is a slight misstep in the wrong direction.[10] Through godly repentance, we quickly find the relief and comfort that comes when we are at peace with the Creator.[11]

Verse 5 says, *"You prepare a table before me in the presence of my enemies; You anoint my head with oil; my cup runs over."*

As we follow in the paths of peace, we find everything in our lives coming into godly order, even as the enemy watches.[12] He has been defeated and can do nothing to hinder the things that God has planned for us. All that we have spiritually hungered for will be provided for us in abundance as we have been transformed from stiff-necked rebellion to easy and quick obedience to God's every word.[13]

Verse 6 says, *"Surely goodness and mercy shall follow me all the days of my life; and I will dwell in the house of the Lord forever."*

As we continue on the paths of peace, we will discover that the goodness of God will cause us to become more and more beautiful in the eyes of our Beloved. His mercy and kindness toward us will never cease, and together the day will come when we will no longer be limited by our flesh, but will enter into our rightful position as glorious heirs of the Kingdom in eternity!

Hallelujah! Let this become fully true in each of our lives![14]

◆ ◆ ◆

Paths of Peace

Though this may seem a unique interpretation of a familiar psalm, it is accurate according to the original Hebrew. Most importantly, however, is the understanding of how important a role peace is to play in our lives as family in God's Kingdom of peace. If our Heavenly Father, Jesus Christ, and the Holy Spirit are our examples of what our spiritual family looks like, then we most certainly must be filled to overflowing with this character trait in our lives.

†

The anointing of peace turns us from stiff-necked rebellion to easy and quick obedience.

When walking this path of peace, there absolutely is no condemnation if we happen to slip off the path momentarily. His mercies are built right into our inheritance. We only need to quickly identify the error, repent, cast out the lie, be refilled with peace, and continue on our way as if it never happened.

Isn't that great news? Why don't we close this final chapter with a fresh refilling of God's peace?

Let's Pray

Dear Heavenly Father,

I stand in awe of Your incredible goodness and mercy toward me at this very moment. From the beginning of time, You have understood the weakness of humankind that I have been subjected to my whole life, but that knowledge has never lessened Your love and affection toward me.

Not only were You aware of my weakness, You through the death and resurrection of Your Son, have planned and made provision available to me so that I can be set free from every weakness. The precious blood of Jesus allows me to wash away the affects of sin in my life, setting me free from all of its effects upon me. The knowledge of this gift has enabled me to walk in complete unity with Your Spirit of peace.

Thank You so much!

Today I choose to once again receive a fresh in-filling of Your Holy Spirit so that Your peaceful waters can bubble up from within, causing me to walk upon the wonderful paths of peace You have laid out for me. I know that Your goodness and loving kindness are pursuing me. A life blessed with Your spiritual abundance is what You have promised me on this earth.

That gift is almost more than I can comprehend!

I ask that You would cause Your glorious peace to shine in me and through me so others may be drawn to the same goodness I have experienced.

In Jesus' name, I pray. Amen.

ENDNOTES

Introduction

1. "Heart Disease and Stroke Statistics—2009 Update," American Heart Association, published December 2008, http://circ.ahajournals.org/cgi/content/short/CIRCULATIONAHA.108.191261v1.

Chapter 1

1. James Strong, *Strong's Exhaustive Concordance of the Bible,* (Peabody, MA: Hendrickson Publishers, 2007). Greek Dictionary, "paraklesis" (# 3874, 3870).

2. *Strong's Exhaustive Concordance,* Hebrew, "shalom" (# 7965).

3. Helen Keller, quoted in *Famous Quotes and Authors,* www.famousquotesandauthors.com/authors/helen_keller_quotes.html; accessed August 4, 2010.

4. Not his real name. Through the book, names of individuals have been changed to protect their identities.

5. Henry W. Wright, *A More Excellent Way: Be in Health* (Thomaston, GA: Pleasant Valley Publications, 2005), xi-xii.

6. *Strong's Exhaustive Concordance,* Greek, "katapausis" (# 2663, 2664, 4520).

Chapter 2

1. Marcus Aurelius, quoted in *Famous Quotes and Authors,* www.famousquotesandauthors.com/authors/marcus_aurelius_quotes.html; accessed August 4, 2010.

2. *Strong's Exhaustive Concordance,* Greek, "harmos" (# 719, 716, 142).

3. *Strong's Exhaustive Concordance,* Greek, "nome" (# 3542, 3551).

4. *Strong's Exhaustive Concordance,* Hebrew, "bachan" (# 974).

5. *Strong's Exhaustive Concordance,* Hebrew, "saraph" (# 8312, 5587, 5586).

Chapter 3

1. *Strong's Exhaustive Concordance,* Greek, "sophronos" (# 4995, 4994, 4998).

2. *Strong's Exhaustive Concordance,* Greek, "sozo" (# 4982).

3. *Strong's Exhaustive Concordance,* Greek, "ochuroma" (# 3794).

4. *Strong's Exhaustive Concordance,* Greek, "logismos" (# 3054, 3164).

5. *Strong's Exhaustive Concordance,* Greek, "kathario" (# 2507, 138).

6. Francois de La Rochefoucauld, quoted in *Famous Quotes and Authors,* www.famousquotesandauthors.com/authors/francois_de_la_rochefoucauld_quotes.html; accessed August 5, 2010.

Chapter 4

1. *Strong's Exhaustive Concordance,* Greek, "hupodeo" (# 5265, 5259).

2. *Strong's Exhaustive Concordance,* Greek, "hetoimasia" (# 2091, 2090, 2092).

3. *Strong's Exhaustive Concordance,* Hebrew, "haah" (# 4998).

4. George MacDonald, quoted in *Famous Quotes and Authors,* http://www.famousquotesandauthors.com/authors/george_macdonald_quotes.html; accessed November 2, 2010.

Chapter 5

1. *Strong's Exhaustive Concordance,* Greek, "phroureo" (# 5432).

2. Jerry W. McCant, quoted in *Famous Quotes and Authors,*

www.famousquotesandauthors.com/topics/peace_of_mind_quotes.html; accessed August 6, 2010.

3. *Strong's Exhaustive Concordance,* Greek, "eirene" (# 1515).

Chapter 6

1. *Strong's Exhaustive Concordance,* Hebrew, "maaseh" (# 4639).

2. Henry Miller, quoted in *Famous Quotes and Authors,* http://www.famousquotesandauthors.com/authors/henry_miller_quotes.html; accessed November 2, 2010.

3. *Strong's Exhaustive Concordance,* Hebrew, "darak" (# 1869).

4. *Strong's Exhaustive Concordance,* Hebrew, "shachal" (# 7826).

5. *Strong's Exhaustive Concordance,* Hebrew, "pethen" (# 6620).

Chapter 7

1. Not his real name.

2. *Strong's Exhaustive Concordance,* Hebrew, "eliy" (# 5940, 5927).

3. *Strong's Exhaustive Concordance,* Hebrew, "Chophniy" (# 2652, 2651).

4. *Strong's Exhaustive Concordance,* Hebrew, "Piynchac" (# 6372).

5. *Strong's Exhaustive Concordance,* Hebrew, "chanak" (# 2596).

6. *Strong's Exhaustive Concordance,* Hebrew, "Iykabowd" (# 350).

7. *Strong's Exhaustive Concordance,* Hebrew, "Yowel" (# 3100).

8. *Strong's Exhaustive Concordance,* Hebrew, "Abiyah" (# 29).

9. Eivind Josef Berggav, quoted in *Famous Quotes and Authors,* www.famousquotesandauthors.com/topics/peace_of_mind_quotes.html; accessed August 6, 2010.

10. *Strong's Exhaustive Concordance,* Greek, "poletes" (# 4163).

11. *Strong's Exhaustive Concordance,* Greek, "paralogizomal" (# 3884).

12. *Strong's Exhaustive Concordance,* Greek, "parakupto" (# 3879).

13. *Strong's Exhaustive Concordance,* Greek, "eleutheria" (# 1657,1658).

14. *Strong's Exhaustive Concordance,* Hebrew, "totsa'ah" (# 8444, 3318).

Chapter 8

1. Not her real name.

2. *Strong's Exhaustive Concordance,* Greek, "pistis" (# 4102).

3. *Strong's Exhaustive Concordance,* Greek, "eirene" (# 1515).

4. John F. Kennedy, quoted in *Famous Quotes and Authors,* www.famousquotesandauthors.com/topics/peace_quotes.html; accessed August 7, 2010.

5. *Strong's Exhaustive Concordance,* Greek, "mastix" (# 3148, 3145).

6. *Strong's Exhaustive Concordance,* Greek, "sozo" (# 4982).

7. *Strong's Exhaustive Concordance,* Greek, "phobeo" (# 5399, 5401).

Chapter 9

1. Eleanor Roosevelt, quoted in *Brainy Quote,* www.brainyquote.com/quotes/topics/topic_peace.html; accessed August 7, 2010.

Chapter 10

1. Thomas à Kempis, quoted in *ThinkExist.com,* http://thinkexist.com/quotes/thomas_kempis/; accessed November 2, 2010.

2. Thomas à Kempis, quoted in *ThinkExist.com*, http://thinkexist.com/quotes/thomas_kempis/2.html; accessed November 2, 2010.

3. *Strong's Exhaustive Concordance,* Greek, "charis (# 5485, 5463).

4. *Strong's Exhaustive Concordance,* Greek, "chara" (# 5479, 5463).

Chapter 11

1. *Strong's Exhaustive Concordance,* Greek, "meteorizo" (# 3349, 3326, 142).

2. *Strong's Exhaustive Concordance,* Hebrew, "gay" (# 1516, 1466).

3. *Strong's Exhaustive Concordance,* Hebrew, "har" (# 2022, 2042).

4. *Strong's Exhaustive Concordance,* Hebrew, "aqallathown" (# 6129, 6127).

5. *Strong's Exhaustive Concordance,* Hebrew, "rekec" (# 7406, 7405).

6. Not her real name.

7. Not his real name.

8. "John Wooden Biography—American Academy of Achievement," http://www.achievement.org/autodoc/page/woo0bio-1; accessed November 2, 2010.

9. John Wooden, quoted in *ThinkExist.com,* thinkexist.com/quotes/with/keyword/peace_of_mind.html; accessed August 7, 2010.

10. "Favorites—Eight Quotes of John Wooden," http://countingmyblessings.typepad.com/weblog/2010/03/favorites-eight-quotes-of-john-wooden.html; accessed November 2, 2010.

11. Dwight L. Moody, quoted in *The Quotable Christian,* www.pietyhilldesign.com/gcq/quotepages/peace.html; accessed August 7, 2010.

12. *Strong's Exhaustive Concordance,* Greek, "pistis" (# 4102, 3982).

Chapter 12

1. *Strong's Exhaustive Concordance,* Hebrew, "ra ah" (# 7462).

2. *Strong's Exhaustive Concordance,* Hebrew, "chacer" (# 2637).

3. *Strong's Exhaustive Concordance,* Hebrew, "shavah" (# 7737).

4. *Strong's Exhaustive Concordance,* Hebrew, "na ah" (# 4999, 4998).

5. *Strong's Exhaustive Concordance,* Hebrew, "rabats" (# 7257); "mayim" (# 4325).

6. *Strong's Exhaustive Concordance,* Hebrew, "nahal" (# 5095).

7. *Strong's Exhaustive Concordance,* Hebrew, "magal" (# 4570).

8. *Strong's Exhaustive Concordance,* Hebrew, "tsedeq" (# 6664, 6667).

9. *Strong's Exhaustive Concordance,* Hebrew, "shebet" (7626).

10. *Strong's Exhaustive Concordance,* Hebrew, "mishenah" (# 4938).

11. *Strong's Exhaustive Concordance,* Hebrew, "nacham" (# 5162).

12. *Strong's Exhaustive Concordance,* Hebrew, "arak" (# 6186); "shulchan" (# 7979).

13. *Strong's Exhaustive Concordance,* Hebrew, "dashen" (# 1878, 1880); "rosh" (# 7218); "shemen" (# 8081).

14. *Strong's Exhaustive Concordance,* Hebrew, "tobe" (# 2896, 2895); "checed" (# 2617).

Reflections

Reflections

Reflections

Reflections

Reflections

Reflections

Reflections

ABOUT MARY TRASK

Contact Mary Trask and learn more about her ministry at:

www.heartreflectionsministies.com
info@heartreflectionsministries.com

To order a copy of *The 12 Gemstones of Revelation,* visit her Website:

http://www.heartreflectionsministries.com

IN THE RIGHT HANDS, THIS BOOK WILL CHANGE LIVES!

Most of the people who need this message will not be looking for this book. To change their lives, you need to put a copy of this book in their hands.

> *But others (seeds) fell into good ground, and brought forth fruit, some a hundred-fold, some sixty-fold, some thirty-fold* (Matthew 13:8).

Our ministry is constantly seeking methods to find the good ground, the people who need this anointed message to change their lives. Will you help us reach these people?

> *Remember this—a farmer who plants only a few seeds will get a small crop. But the one who plants generously will get a generous crop* (2 Corinthians 9:6).

EXTEND THIS MINISTRY BY SOWING
3 BOOKS, 5 BOOKS, 10 BOOKS, OR MORE TODAY,
AND BECOME A LIFE CHANGER!

Thank you,

Don Nori Sr., Publisher
Destiny Image
Since 1982